The Sequel To Everything

The Case Histories

A Further Exploration of the Way in Which the Soul Talks Through the Body

By Chris Thomas & Diane Baker

www.capallbann.co.uk

The Sequel to Everything

©2001 Chris Thomas & Diane Baker

First printed 2001

Reprinted 2003

ISBN 1861631375

Cover design by Paul Mason

Published by:

Capall Bann Publishing
Auton Farm
Milverton
Somerset
TA4 1NE

We would like to dedicate this book to all of our clients. It is from them that we have learned the workings of the body and the soul

We would also like to dedicate this book to everyone who has broken their brainwashing by the medical profession and sought to find their own answers. To these people belongs the truth.

Contents

Introduction

The publication of "*Everything You Always Wanted To Know About Your Body But, So Far Nobody's Been Able To Tell You*" generated a great deal of interest in what is, to most people, a new way of looking at the body and how illness is generated. As it is such a new way of looking, we have been asked to put together a collection of case histories to help understand how the symptoms can be read and how to make more sense of the body and soul's messages.

We have also been asked to describe the work that we do and how these answers were arrived at, this is covered in chapter one.

All of the case histories given in the following chapters are genuine. They are all clients who have consulted us in our psychic surgery practice over the past few years. Everyone who comes to us is guaranteed full confidentiality and so we have not given names, just symptoms and their basic background where relevant to their symptoms. Where appropriate, we have also given the suggestions we gave to the client for their "homework".

At first glance, the concepts raised in "Everything..etc" sound very complicated, but they need not be. All that is really required is an alteration in focus and understanding of the workings of the body and the way in which the soul, the consciousness, and the body are inextricably linked together.

If you have read "Everything..etc" you will understand how the links work and the way in which the chakras play a major part in our lives and our well being. But, for those who have not read the first book, there is a brief description of the soul/chakra/body connection in the second chapter. The remainder of this book then describes the ways in which the symptoms of an illness can be tracked back to its root cause and the "homework" given to help deal with these root cause issues.

There are also a couple of case histories which demonstrate that if we ask the body to generate a specific condition, it will oblige with the appropriate symptoms.

We have also included some further past life case histories to help demonstrate that not all health problems relate to our current lives. As this is probably the last book we will be writing on these issues, we have also included a section of some of our more unusual cases.

Most importantly of all, we all need to recognise the fact that illness is not a punishment of any kind, from any source. Nor is illness a "test", an obstacle, to be struggled against and overcome. Illness is a message from our own soul trying to tell us that we have taken a step in the wrong direction - no more than that. There is no mystery nor any religious connotations to this process, just very simple, usually literal, messages to try to help us to understand ourselves and our lives. All that we need to do to heal any illness is to re-learn how to read the body's messages and take some simple corrective actions.

It is this simple.

The description of the chakras and their connections with the physical body were first "mapped" at least seven thousand years ago by the Sumerians as they were developing their Ayurvedic practices (Ayurvedic is a Sanskrit word which has been translated to mean "The Science of Life"). What we have done is to work with these concepts and develop them into a more day to day understanding of the workings of the body. In order to achieve this, one of us works as a "psychic surgeon" with the ability to "scan" the body to see what is actually occurring physically and energetically and to track the body's energies back to their source. By using this scanning ability, it has been possible to track the energies of the body and follow their interaction with the physical body and to trace illness back to its originating cause. It is also possible to "read" DNA using these techniques and often correct the memories of past life trauma that so called genetic defects usually are.Contrary to most medical thinking, our genetic structures are actually our primary memory system where everything we have ever been is remembered.

The purpose of this book is to help to understand how the body really functions and how to track illnesses back to their originating source. The chakras, as a diagnostic tool, are totally foolproof once you have learned how to read them. The body is also quite literal in what it is trying to say to us. The "old wives" (the village wise woman) expressions of "I was so angry, I could feel my gall rising"; "I was so frustrated, I just had to vent my spleen"; "get it off your chest" all mean what they say and reflect the fact that we once understood the workings of the body much more intimately than we do today. The practices of western material medicine have divorced us from our bodies and our understanding of the mechanisms of illness. By re-learning how the soul uses the body to tell us of our wanderings from our intended path in life, we can all begin to heal ourselves of any and all ailments regardless of how serious they might appear to be. If we can take responsibility for our ills and set about correcting the route we took in our lives to generate those ills, we can all return to a state of perfect health.

We can all heal ourselves, we just need to re-learn how to read the body.

Chapter One

Psychic Surgery

The method of working we use is called "psychic surgery". There are several different versions of what this type of approach constitutes. Essentially, it breaks down into two distinct practices, namely intrusive and non-intrusive.

Intrusive psychic surgery is where the hands of the psychic surgeon pass through the skin of the patient and a medical procedure performed inside the patient's body. This is the type of psychic surgery carried out mainly in the Philippines and Brazil.

Non-intrusive psychic surgery is where the same procedures are carried out but the hands of the psychic surgeon remain outside of the body. This type is usually carried out in the west and is the type we practice mainly because passing our hands through the body of a client would scare the life out of us never mind our client! Filipino and Brazilian cultures are more prepared to accept the intrusive type of work whilst we in the west are somewhat more squeamish. Historically, intrusive psychic surgery was carried out under Celtic shamanism but this was stopped by the Christian church and has rarely been practised in the west since.

There are fundamental differences between the two schools but also fundamental similarities.In the west, we have adopted a very materialistic, physical view of the world where the concept of psychic surgery, or any kind of energetic healing, is extremely difficult to grasp, however, there is a rational explanation.

Let us start with one universally accepted fact - all matter is energy. What this means is that everything we "see" as solid, physical matter is actually comprised of energy. We only think that matter is solid because our brains are tuned to accept particular frequencies of energy in that way. The same is true of the human body. Our brains are tuned to the frequencies of energy which comprise the body and see it as dense, solid material but, underneath it all, it is still energy.

In the east they have called this bodily energy "Qi" (pronounced chi) whilst in the Hindu, Ayurvedic, traditions it is called "Prahna". We have no word for it in the west other than the consciousness or, possibly, "soul". Our preference would be for consciousness as the word soul has many religious connotations which mean very different things to different people. In this sense, consciousness can be defined in the same way as Qi or Prahna, that is, life force.

This life force, consciousness, has many functions within our lives but its first function is to construct the "physical" body. There are many schools of thought and religious concepts which surround the conception and birth process and we do not have any argument with any of them. Our own researches have been into the "mechanical" process involved. Whatever the ultimate source of life an individual holds to be true, there is a process undergone to bring that life force into the "physical" realms.

The process is this.The individual's consciousness approaches the egg fertilised by the parents. As the consciousness begins to interact with the egg, it draws together the energies it requires to construct the various organs and structures and condenses them into their new body form, the so-called "etheric template". This template provides the blueprint into which the skeleton, organs, etc fit. Each component of the body has its own energy frequency and the template draws these frequencies to their appropriate location.

The consciousness then triggers appropriate DNA sequences to bring these organs to their full function (see chapter seven for how past life memories can be built into the new body at this stage in our development).It is the etheric template which makes all of us the same but it is the consciousness (and its genetic memories) which makes each of us a unique individual.

All of these various energies remain within the body and keep it functioning throughout our lives. The consciousness is present within the body and is represented by the seven primary chakras. Bodily energies, and therefore its physical integrity, are distributed from the chakras to their corresponding organs by the "meridians".

The word chakra is originally Sanskrit and has been translated as meaning "spinning wheel of light", this is what the chakra actually looks like from the front, a rotating wheel. From the side they look like a funnel, or to give it its correct name, a vortex. The meridians are energy "conduits" which look a little like fibre optic cables and criss cross the body distributing the primary energies of the chakras. The flow of energy within the meridians is the principle behind acupuncture.

The range of energy frequencies contained within the body are immense. Our own researches would give them a frequency range of between 7.56 cycles per second, at their lowest, to approximately 70,000 cycles per second at their highest. This is the range of energies generated within the physical body by the consciousness and is sufficient to build all of the components of the body. It might appear anomalous to describe this form of energy in these terms but without any kind of reference point for "consciousness energy", we can only relate it to a standard means of measurement.

These energies and their functions are more fully described in two of our previous books, *The Journey Home* and *The Fool's First Steps*.

Illness arises because we have disrupted these energies in some way causing one of the organs or bodily systems to be deficient in energy and their integrity and function begins to suffer. This is why hands on healing and acupuncture can be very successful in healing physical illness as they can help correct the imbalance of energies. Acupuncture works in a "mechanical" way by unblocking the meridians affected whilst healing works in a more energetic way by "topping up" the energy deficiency.

The Filipino Christian Spiritist healers (intrusive psychic surgery) have a belief that the energy for their healing work comes from the concept of "Spirit Protectors" who are directed in their work by Jesus The Christ. This is a common view held by very many healers world wide and stems from the healer's religious beliefs as much as any other reality. We have not met any Moslem healers but, for the same reasons, we are sure that they would believe that their healing capabilities come from Allah.

Whilst we would not doubt their belief systems and we certainly would not deny or even doubt the existence of "spirit protectors" or spirit helpers of many kinds, there is a process at work from which these healing energies stem and the spirit helpers only help to direct or enhance the basic energy source. The originating energy source is the healer's own consciousness.

To understand this statement, we have to turn to a new branch of mathematics. These maths were developed by the

North American Space Agency (NASA) to understand the forces at work within massive revolving objects, such as planets, whilst they were still revolving. Up until now, the way scientists worked out the forces involved in a moving object was to freeze the object in time and space and calculate what is happening whilst it was at rest, a situation which does not occur in nature and gives a very false view of the realities of the forces involved.

This new maths, called The Mathematics of a Revolving Sphere, addresses this problem and came up with some very interesting conclusions. Essentially, what these mathematical proofs imply is that we are considerably more than we ever thought. The human consciousness spans a great many dimensions and our activities on Earth make use of the energy potential contained within these other dimensions. When their original proofs and findings were first published, they could "prove" the existence of 29 dimensions with the implication that there were many more beyond these.

We would define a dimension as being a marker point along a line of energy frequencies which incorporate the frequencies of energy above the last dimensional marker but below the next.

So, how can this mathematical theory apply to healing? In a very real way this theory actually gives us a working model for the consciousness.

Our findings on the energy frequencies contained within the physical body are given above but, the consciousness itself extends beyond the physical into what has become known as "The Higher Self". The Higher Self is the range of energy frequencies encompassed by the total consciousness but which cannot be contained within the restricted confines of the physical body. What we do as individuals is first determined by the Higher Self and we act out the wishes of these higher realms of our consciousness. These higher realms extend the energy potential of our consciousness to as far as 250,000 cycles per second and can incorporate up to 42 dimensions.

We know how strange this concept sounds but after nearly twenty years researching the subject, they are the only conclusions that can be reached.

This energy potential, contained within the total consciousness, gives us the source for the energies that are produced out of a healer's hands. The best way to describe this process is to use an analogy.

Think about how a light bulb works. Energy is supplied into the filament of the bulb by the electricity flowing along the electric cable. The atoms of the filament receive this extra energy and some of the electrons revolving around the nucleus become energised and move up to the next energy band of the atom. These electrons cannot stay at this higher energy level as it would fundamentally alter the material from which the filament is made and the electron has to "dump" the extra energy in order to return to its original energy band within the atom. As this extra energy is released, it gives us the light. This process continues for as long as the electricity flows and appears to be a continuous process as our brains cannot register the speed at which the process is occurring.

Healing works in a very similar way. The healer is faced with a healing problem and the consciousness of the healer "walks" across the energy potential contained within the healer's total consciousness and releases the energy for the healing work in hand. As someone who can "see" and read energies, this is a process observed very many times whilst working with other healers.

Most people, including healers, have sought to wrap the healing process in mystery but it really is this simple a process. Mysticism has traditionally been used as a way of covering up the lack of knowledge of the participants and it is time that the realities and beautiful simplicity of the healing process was brought into the open.

The work that a psychic surgeon can do takes the simple healing process many steps further. It does not matter if the psychic surgeon works intrusively or non-intrusively, the process is identical.

Essentially, what makes a psychic surgeon a psychic surgeon, as opposed to a healer, is an ability to alter the way in which the brain perceives the physical/energetic nature of the body. In other words, the psychic surgeon has retrained their brain into seeing beyond the body's physical density and into its energetic construction. Some, such as ourselves, have taken this re-tuning a stage further and can "see" the body's energies at work. This view is a little like a medical MRI scanner but in real time. Once the energy, gathered across the multidimensional self, has arrived at the hands, the psychic surgeon manipulates the energy to carry out tasks which can mimic medical surgery.

There is no real mystery in this process, it is a question of re-tuning the senses in a particular way to be able to receive and manipulate available energies. There is, of course, a huge variation in the way each psychic surgeon works. We are all individuals and each of us work in ways suitable to our own life experiences and the intent we bring to the healing process. Some work with non-physical "entities", such as spirit protectors or spirit guides etc, whilst others do not. It is a matter of personal preference and personal experience.

To describe how this process works, we can use the example of a gall stone removal.

The psychic surgeon is consulted by a client who has a medical diagnosis of a gall stone (third chakra - suppressed anger). The psychic surgeon will take this information and confirm it themselves by carrying out their own "scan" of the condition in their own way. From this information, they will begin to gather together the energy frequencies which correspond to the elements of the body connected with the proposed removal. In other words, the energy of the skin, the muscles, the gall bladder and the gall stone. Once the energy collection is complete, they will continue in a method appropriate to their own way of working.

The intrusive type of psychic surgeon will register in their minds that the skin is a layer of dense energy and that their hand is of a similar density. This allows the hand to become "transparent" and pass through the skin very simply and easily as they are not physical barriers. Once through the skin and muscles, the outer layers of the gall bladder will be passed through in the same way. The gall stone is also constructed of energy and can, therefore, be easily contained within the energy field generated around the psychic surgeon's hand. The psychic surgeon has already tuned their hand to accept the energy of the gall stone, if they had not, the hand would simply pass through the stone without effect. Once the stone is in their hand, they simply reverse the process and bring the hand back through the skin.

What the observer sees is the psychic surgeon's hand pass through the skin and return with the gall stone in the hand. The observer's brain is not tuned to the energy of the body in the same way as the psychic surgeon's is, but to the physical density of the skin and the gall stone. The psychic surgeon sees the the stone as energy but the observer sees it as dense, physical material.

A non intrusive psychic surgeon, the type practised by us, works in very much the same way. The difference is that they do not pass their hand through the skin but remove the gall stone by dissipating the energy of the stone. The stone does not actually appear in the visible, physical spectrum of energy frequencies but is effectively dissolved on an energetic level within the body.

It all sounds quite complicated but all that really happens is that the psychic surgeon understands the underlying energetic nature of the body and has developed ways of manipulating those energies to perform apparent miracles.

In the last couple of years, we have seen the beginnings of a change in the way in which the consciousness interacts with the physical body. As our interaction with the consciousness changes, the body is also changing and there are increasing incidents of the medical profession being unable to treat illness. This is a reflection of the fact that the energies within the body are actually increasing and the nature of the physical is rapidly changing.

For more about these changes, see chapter eight.

Chapter Two

The Mechanism of Illness

All illnesses have a root cause. There is no such thing as an accidental illness. Illness comes about because we have, somewhere along the line, taken a slightly wrong turn and the consciousness (soul) is trying to tell us that we need to take a look at our lives and begin to correct our behaviour and our attitude towards ourselves.

The symptoms of illness are many and varied. They can range from a mild cold to a heart attack, from a cut finger to Crohn's disease. All symptoms. All add up to a condition where action is required to alleviate the symptoms. But, symptoms are just that, symptoms. They are the body's way of saying that a problem has arisen and it requires some help and attention in order to help it return to its normal condition.

When we are healthy we tend not to think about the body too much and certainly not why it is healthy. It is only when something goes wrong that we pay it any attention. This is what illness is, the body's way of saying there is a problem. How we address the problem determines how quickly we return to a state of health and the side effects we encounter along the way. What the body and the soul is really asking us to do is to try to understand why the symptoms arose in the first place. What the soul does not want us to do is to rush off to the nearest doctor for a pill to mask its messages (the symptoms).

Think of a car. If we are driving along and the oil warning light comes on we know that there is a problem within the engine. It is a mechanical way of saying that the engine requires some assistance. We have two choices. We either pay attention and try to discover why and where the problem arose or we can cut the wire that runs from the engine to the warning light. Most of us would argue that cutting the wire would not be a very sensible way to proceed and yet this is what most of us do with an illness. By taking a medicine or a remedy without understanding why we became ill, why our warning light was switched on, we are not being very sensible. Yet this is what we do when symptoms arise - we take something to mask the symptoms, cut the warning wire, without investigating why we have the symptoms in the first place.There is another way.

We are used to the expression "body and soul". What we need to do is begin to take a new look at what is meant by this expression. This is not a religious viewpoint nor is this chapter going to end up saying that your illness is a punishment from "God". What it is going to do is to redefine this expression and explain what it means and why it has a relevance to the symptoms of illness.So, let us start by changing the words a little.

We are a consciousness. It is this consciousness which makes us a complete individual. So, instead of the word "soul" we can substitute the word consciousness. Consciousness can be defined in several ways but its real definition is that which makes me me and you you. What this consciousness does is to build for itself a physical body, the ones that we inhabit. This sounds a little strange to begin with but there are ways of explaining this which can, hopefully, make the concept a little easier to understand.

The consciousness is an energy. We do not have a specific word to define this kind of energy and this is why the word soul is all encompassing and why it means different things to different people. Underlying all scientific proof and theory is the model provided by the scientist Albert Einstein who proved that all matter (the physical world, rocks, trees, plants, bodies, etc) is comprised of energy. In this way, although the world around us appears to be solid it is, in fact, made of energy. This is how the consciousness, the soul, builds the body. It combines together a number of different frequencies of energy to bring about the physical body.

This is what the expression "body and soul" really means. We are not a body that has a soul, a consciousness, but a soul that has built for itself a body.

The scientists are aware that there is a consciousness at work within the body but have been unable to place it. The problem is that looking at the physical body to find the energy that drives it is like looking at a light bulb and trying to see the electricity. What we really need to do is to try to look beyond the purely physical and see the energy at work beneath.

To understand how this consciousness (soul) energy interacts with the body, we have to look back to a time in the further reaches of recorded history.

Understanding The Route Map

To begin to understand the mechanism of any illness, we first have to take a fundamentally new look at the body and the way in which it is constructed. We are not talking about any kind of mystery, mysticism or religion, but a return to the ancient wisdoms which brought us herbalism, acupuncture, aromatherapy, reflexology, etc, a return to the basic philosophies which underlie all Eastern and Western healing traditions (including current western medical practices).

The workings of the body were first investigated at least 7 000 years ago by the Sumerians. The Sumerians developed a number of approaches to healing illness. All of these approaches were grouped together under the term "Ayurveda". This is a word which, in Sanskrit, means "The Science of Life". This was a completely "whole body" approach. They developed many different techniques and practices to deal with illnesses in ways appropriate to each individual. Most of these techniques are still carried on today in most parts of the world.

For example, the Asian Indian tradition of Ayurvedic Medicine is a direct descendent of this whole body approach. Eastern traditions which work with the body's "meridians" have stemmed from the same origin. Herbalism, in all of its many forms and traditions, are a continuation of the Sumerian practices. All western drugs have also been derived from these herbal traditions.So, the Sumerians can be seen as the originators of all healing.

However, one Sumerian discovery underlies all of the others. All "physical" material is comprised of atoms and all atoms are comprised of energy. We do not see this energy with our direct vision because our brains are "tuned" to see and sense these clusters of atoms as solid, physical material.

This means that the body is ultimately comprised of energy. This is the kind of energy which underlies all living things. This energy known as "Pranah" or "Qi" depending upon which tradition you adopt or, as we would define it, consciousness, performs a huge variety of functions within the body.

The first is to provide a "template" for the "physical" tissue to form itself around, the so-called "etheric template". The second is to provide an energy flow around the body, into and out of the organs, known as the meridians. There is also a primary source of these energies within the body, the chakras. Many interpretations have been put onto the chakras, their locations and functions, over the centuries but it is only in

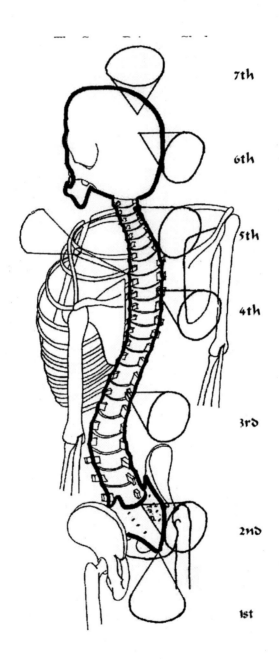

7th

6th

5th

4th

3rd

2nd

1st

recent years that we are beginning to rediscover their real function and the role that they play in the body's well being.

The Chakras

In the west, we are beginning to become increasingly aware of the chakras. Unfortunately, in the translation from the eastern tradition into the western interpretation, many misunderstandings have arisen.

The original "mapping" of the chakras by the Sumerians, and the description of their role in our health, was, essentially, very simple. By bringing them into our western understanding they have become unnecessarily complicated and infused with a certain degree of mystery and mysticism. We seem to have a need to complicate matters in the west, especially when it comes to health problems.

If we return to the original understanding the whole concept becomes much more easily understood. There are seven primary chakras. These are the ones you will see on posters and wall charts depicting the chakras. Each of the seven chakras relates to an element of our personality and every day lives and each of these elements link very directly to the organs within the body. The interpretation of the messages from the chakras and through the body is also quite literal. We do not need to look for any complexity in our interpretation, just begin to understand ourselves and our bodies in newer, simpler ways.

There is a great deal of scepticism attached to the role the chakras play in the health of the body but, before you stop reading, read the descriptions of the chakras and the organs to which they relate and think of someone you know who has an illness. From what you know of that person and their illness, link the illness to the associated chakra and see how accurate the interpretation actually is. We think you will be pleasantly surprised.

The chakras are the consciousness made physical and all seven chakras are located along the spine. The first is at the very base of the spine, the bottom of the coccyx. The second is located where the spine meets the pelvis. The third is located just above the tummy button. The fourth is located at the level of the heart. The fifth is located in the throat, mid way between the Adams apple and the chin. The sixth is located in the centre of the forehead, just above the bridge of the nose and the seventh is located at the very top of the head. As the chakras extend away from the body, they form the aura.

Each of the chakras relate to who we are as unique individuals and how we interact with the world and people around us.

The First Chakra

The first chakra links us into the physical world and is, therefore, directly concerned with our sense of security. It deals with the physical structures of the body: the skin, the muscles and the skeleton. It also links directly with the kidneys and the urinary system and also aspects of the adrenal glands. An interpretation of health problems linked into this chakra will, therefore, relate to these organs or regions.

For example, if we feel stressed (mildly insecure) in a situation, at work for example, we will begin to feel tension in some of the muscles. If this kind of situation becomes prolonged, the skeleton can become affected. Skeletal problems tend to arise in response to long term stress or insecurity arising from that stress.

If we feel insecure within situations which have a more immediate outcome, the kidneys and adrenal glands will become affected, leading to an increased need to urinate. Children and the elderly, in particular, tend to suffer from these kinds of problems.

A method of interpretation for first, or root, chakra problems is this: skin problems (such as eczema) are all about "I am feeling fairly insecure in this situation and I am letting you know that I would like some help". Muscle problems are to do with "I am feeling mildly insecure and am becoming quite stressed about it". Skeletal problems are long term insecurities "I have been feeling mildly insecure for a long time and I am beginning to resent it". Kidney and urinary problems are to do with "I am feeling very insecure within this immediate situation and I do not know whether to run away or stay".

It sounds very simplistic but why try to make a straightforward problem complicated? Ways of healing these problems include: increasing the amount of practical things we do such as walking, using our hands for handicrafts, etc; increasing our level of self confidence by taking assertiveness classes etc.

The Second Chakra

The second chakra (also known as the sacral chakra) has two functions. Its primary function is our creativity. Its secondary function is connected to our sexual relationships. Because of this relationship link, it relates to the reproductive organs. These are: the ovaries, uterus, cervix and fallopian tubes in women and the testicles, prostate, penis and scrotum in men. All problems associated with any dysfunction within these organs will stem from either a lack of creativity in our lives or from some kind of relationship problem.

All of the health problems associated with these organs can be healed by working with the chakra's primary function, creativity. Taking up a creative hobby can clear these problems. This is especially true where the problem has arisen from a relationship issue and it cannot be resolved very easily.

The Thíro Chakra

The third chakra (also known as the solar plexus chakra) relates to two elements of our lives. Its primary function is with personal power issues and its secondary function is with the emotions. It interacts directly with all of the abdominal organs. These are: the liver, the gall bladder, the pancreas, the spleen, the stomach and the large and small intestines.

Personal power issues are situations where your ideas or views are taken seriously by others. If they are not, emotions can arise which will begin to affect the associated organ.

The liver deals with fear, jealousy and guilt. The gall bladder with unexpressed anger. The pancreas with the "force" we use to express our emotions (if we should have reacted strongly to a situation and all we did was turn away without response, the unexpressed force of response lodges in the pancreas). The spleen deals with frustration, particularly frustration connected with suppressed anger. The stomach deals with situations where we had to "swallow" our views and accept those of others, quite literally situations we could not "stomach". The intestines, both large and small, deal with the emotional "rubbish" we are hanging on to and need to let go of.

As all of the above work with the digestive system in one way or another, it should become clear why diets do not work. Unless the underlying emotion is cleared, weight will always return. The same is true for cellulite. Cellulite is caused by the lymphatic tissue in the legs and buttocks becoming blocked. The lower body lymph tissue is controlled by the spleen. If you have not dealt with some of the frustrations in your life, cellulite will not go away.

The best way of sorting out these problems is to deal with the situation as it arose, if it was not possible to do so, the next best option is with the "giveaway" (see the next chapter).

The Fourth Chakra

The fourth chakra (also known as the heart chakra) also has two functions. Its primary function is to connect the "higher" elements of our consciousness with our physical bodies. Its secondary function deals with how we express love, either for ourselves or towards others.

The chakra works with the heart, blood and circulation; the immune system (especially the thymus gland); and the endocrine system (this is the body's hormone control system). Problems with these systems arise because we have difficulty expressing love either for ourselves or for others.

Problems with the heart and circulation tend to occur because we have difficulty expressing our love towards others, or sometimes towards ourselves - literally hardening our hearts. This tends to occur when we become locked into particular patterns of behaviour and ignore the wants and needs of those around us. Heart disease, which is increasingly common, is related to this aspect of our lives but there are several other factors involved such as the rise in hysterectomy operations and free radicals in our diet (especially in vegetable fats and oils - see chapter twelve).

Problems with the immune system tend to arise when we ignore our own needs. The thymus gland controls the function of the upper body lymphatic tissue. If we have difficulty "loving" ourselves (honouring ourselves), the lymph tissue blocks and many problems can occur. The extreme form of these problems is breast cancer.

We have a huge capacity to love so it is important that we share this equally between ourselves and others. There is no substitute for re-learning how to love.

The Fifth Chakra

The fifth chakra (sometimes known as the throat chakra) also has two functions. Its primary is self expression and its secondary is communication. It works directly with the mouth, teeth, lungs and bronchial channels, the throat, with the metabolism (especially the thyroid gland) and the parathyroid (a small gland embedded in the thyroid which controls the body's calcium balance).

Problems with the lungs tend to arise because we are not expressing our thoughts and wants adequately.

Problems with the thyroid can arise because we feel that we are being prevented from expressing our thoughts and wants. If you cannot "get it off your chest" for yourself, the only recourse is to use the giveaway.

The Sixth Chakra

The sixth chakra's (also sometimes known as the third eye chakra) primary function is with our "spirituality" and psychic vision. Its secondary function is with the physical senses. It links directly with the ears, the nose, the left eye, the lower brain and central nervous system, and with the pituitary gland (a small pea shaped gland at the base of the brain which controls the production of a number of hormones). Problems with these senses tend to arise because we have decided, for whatever reason, to detach ourselves from the world around us. For example, deafness can arise because our partner chatters a great deal. Simplistic as it sounds, we will always shut out the things we do not want to see, hear, taste, smell, touch because we wish to live in a world of our own making or because the world around us has become too much for us to bear.

The only effective way of dealing with these kinds of problems is to learn to accept our place in the world and change our intent and be an active part of humanity and re-open our senses. Realising and accepting that we have psychic capabilities, and making use of them, will also override any problems with the physical senses. This does not mean becoming a Tarot card reader, just using our natural intuition.

The Seventh Chakra

The seventh chakra (also known as the crown chakra) is the energetic link with the higher elements of our being. These higher elements have several names which include the soul, the consciousness, the higher self, etc. The seventh chakra links these elements of the self into the energetic structures of the physical body. This is not the same link as the fourth chakra. That link is into the workings of the physical body, this link is into the body's total energy systems.

The seventh chakra links into the right eye, the upper brain (the subconscious mind) and with the pineal gland (a small gland at the base of the brain which produces melatonin, a hormone concerned with sleep and the production of the body's own natural antioxidants).

Problems connected with the seventh chakra are quite rare, but one notable illness is ME (or Chronic Fatigue Syndrome). ME occurs when we have ignored the promptings of our "higher" consciousness elements and the body, through the pineal gland and its melatonin, is put onto hold until we begin to resolve some of our deeper issues.

So, as you can see, the body is not just a collection of parts but an interdependent whole. The range of energies contained within the physical body are immense. Illness arises because we have not quite carried out the wishes of the consciousness. If we listen to our bodies, and therefore our soul, we can undo all illness.

Whilst this statement is true and all illnesses can be traced back to our emotional responses to a given situation, there can be aggravating factors which can make health problems potentially very much more serious. If we have generated a weakness within a chakra and it has been transferred into an organ or system, this weakness can be made worse by outside factors. Our food contains many harmful chemicals, our water is saturated with pharmaceutical drugs residues and farm chemicals, our whole environment is filled with artificial hormones. For example. There is one skin condition which has seen a dramatic increase in recent years and that is skin cancer.

Skin cancer occurs when the cell structures of the skin become overloaded with an outside stimulus. Most people put the rise in this condition down to breaks in the ozone layer. Whilst this is a contributory factor, it does not appear to be the cause. The cause seems to lie with the vast quantity of artificial oestrogens in our environment blocking the melanin receptors in the skin cells. These artificial oestrogens are found in the pill, HRT, plastic bottles, food animals, etc and are not removed from our water supplies as the current water treatments do not remove pharmaceutical residues. Melanin is the reactive hormone within skin cells which darken the skin colour after exposure to sunshine. Skin cells contain oestrogen receptors which keep the skin moist and supple. If these receptors become blocked with artificial oestrogen, the melanin cannot respond correctly and a melanoma can result.

All of these external factors add up to make these chakra weaknesses into a greater problem than would normally be the case. If we can begin to treat our bodies with respect and understanding and only put into it the substances it needs, respond honestly to those around us, then all illnesses can be prevented from occurring and any existing illness "cured".

These are not idle statements. The body wants to heal itself, all we have to do is listen to it.It is never too late to begin!

Incidentally, the traditional colours given for the chakras, red, orange, yellow, green, blue, indigo and violet, are not chosen just because they are pretty colours. If you look at a scientific demonstration of how colour changes with variations of energy frequency, you will find the same sequence of colours. These are the colours which will be produced when you shine white light through a glass prism or sunlight through rain to produce a rainbow.

Colour is a function of the frequencies of energy. Our brains are tuned to these frequencies in order for us to see in normal daylight, the visible spectrum. As we rise through the energy spectrum's visible frequencies we see, in sequence, the following colours in turn:

Red, Orange, Yellow, Green, Blue, Indigo, Violet.

We cannot see frequencies below red or above violet with the human eye.

However, as we undergo our change in consciousness, new energies are being made available to us. As we integrate the higher aspects of who we are into the physical aspects of our consciousness, the colours of the chakras change. We are currently so far down this route of change that the old colours, the red, orange, yellow, green etc. no longer apply. The whole of the human etheric template is now constructed of the new chakra energies and their colours have changed accordingly.

> The first chakra is now a copper gold with "flashes" of clear gold, violet and petrol blue.

> The second chakra is petrol blue with flashes of clear gold, violet and copper gold.

> The third chakra is petrol green with flashes of clear gold, violet and petrol blue.

The fourth chakra is now transparent with random flecks of all of the colours.

The fifth chakra is also transparent but with a lesser number of coloured flecks.

The sixth chakra is the same as the fifth with an even lesser number of coloured flecks.

The seventh chakra is transparent. Totally pure energy.

For more about the changes of energy, see chapter eight.

Chapter Three

Case Histories

Straightforward Cases

The next few chapters detail a number of case histories from our files which are intended to help you understand how to read your symptoms and relate them to the appropriate chakra or chakras. To illustrate how we arrive at our determination of a client's health problem, we thought it would be helpful to take you through a typical healing session. Our healing sessions take approximately one and one half hours during which time we discuss the symptoms and how our client's life has been and is now, to try to tell the full story of how their symptoms arose.

We start by taking a full medical history, all known symptoms, medical procedures undergone, medication, when symptoms started and what the client feels about their condition and their medical diagnosis.

Following this, Chris "scans" their body to "read" the energies of the chakras and organs etc. By reading the chakras in this way it is possible to determine which organs are not functioning correctly. By not functioning we mean the energies of a particular organ are not in balance and so one, or more, of the functions of the organ are not performing at their "normal" level. From this scan we can look at regions of the client's life which have brought about the chakra and organ energy imbalances and help them to understand the root cause issues.

We then "clean out" the chakras and organs of their energy imbalances and restructure the energies of the body.

Whilst this is going on, Di talks with the client about the issues raised from the scan and helps them to work out ways of overcoming particular problems if they are still ongoing or ways of clearing out the residue of the problem from their system if the issues are a left over from the past, in other words, the client's "homework". Although the cleansing and re-balancing work we do can be extremely effective in cleansing problems out of the system, there will always be issues which we cannot clean out as they are issues which the client has to deal with for themselves.

To clean everything out of a client's system would mean that we would have to take full responsibility for our client's lives and whilst this can, sometimes, be very tempting to attempt, we really cannot take on this level of responsibility.

Other than the repair work, our aim is that our clients leave us with a cleansed and balanced energy system and a greater understanding of how their health problems arose in the first place. They should also have an understanding of how to deal with their issues for themselves which can help them prevent any health problems from re-occurring in the future. Knowledge and understanding really is power when it comes to health issues.

We cannot stress strongly enough that symptoms of ill health arise because we have travelled in a direction which our consciousness (soul) considers to be inappropriate. Illness arises for no other cause. To prevent symptoms arising, we must deal with the situations we encounter in life in ways which are appropriate for us as individuals. This involves "speaking our truth" on all levels, be it personal power issues or our thoughts and ideas. Each situation we encounter in life is there to be dealt with, not walked away from. The more we walk away, the quicker we will develop symptoms of ill health. The more we deal with those kinds of situations, the longer we stay in good health. It is this simple!

However, we do, sometimes, encounter situations where it is not appropriate or not possible to express ourselves fully. In these instances, the alternative is to make use of "homework". Our homework suggestions usually include making use of the "giveaway". This is a process first used by North American Indians to help clear out emotional problems. The process is very simple but can be extremely effective. The giveaway can involve a variety of approaches but the most effective is to write down all of your thoughts and, especially, feelings about specific events in your life that you feel have not been cleared or dealt with properly (they amount to the root cause of a health problem). DO NOT READ YOUR WRITING BACK as this takes the emotion back into your system but, once you have finished writing, tear up the paper and either dispose of it in the bin or, preferably, burn it. This method works for every situation.

If you know who has brought about particular situations, the giveaway can be modified slightly and you can write that person, or persons, a letter. Address the letter to them, it does not matter if they are alive or dead, and write all that you would have liked to have said to them at the time but did not. Again, do not read your writing back, just rip it up and dispose of it. You can, of course, send them the letter if you prefer as this can help them to understand how they hurt you and can clear the air properly.

It is easy to be sceptical about such a simple process, but it really does work. There is now even medical research which supports the view that this process is very effective at unlocking emotional trauma and assisting in the recovery from a range of health problems.

If you do not want to write, you can paint the problem and dispose of it in the same way. Alternatively, if you are used to visualisation exercises during your meditations, you can travel inwards into the body and ask each organ, in turn, to tell you what it is hanging on to. Any unwanted emotions or memories can then be wrapped up in a gold "bubble" and removed from the body.

Other homework suggestions include drinking organic red wine to help cleanse the blood. Grape seeds contain a substance called olygomeric proanthocyanidin which is an active antioxidant. When the grape seeds are crushed for wine making, this ingredient is released into the wine. Red grape juice also contains this ingredient but not in as high a concentration as in wine. If you do not drink alcohol, the grape juice is almost as effective. Unfortunately, white wine does not contain the active ingredient as the seeds are usually removed from the grape during the fermentation process. Organic red wine is best as it does not contain any pesticides or any of the other chemicals found in commercial crops.

Where there are bacterial infections within the gut, we have found that a couple of measures of neat vodka can help a great deal in clearing the bacteria without harm or removing useful bacteria. The usual dosage we recommend is one large measure of neat vodka per night for two or three nights. We have found that this is usually sufficient for most infections. Again, if you do not drink alcohol or cannot drink neat spirits, there is an alternative in grapefruit seed extract (trade name Citricidal - see chapter twelve). This is an immensely powerful natural antibiotic reputed to be fifty times more powerful than tea tree oil, so read the label very carefully before taking it.

We have also suggested eating more organic chocolate, staying in bed with a good book when you are not ill, smashing old plates and crockery to taking up a creative hobby. We try to give good homework!

Case One
A man in his early thirties.

Medical History:
Asthma attacks began at about age twelve which has left a weakness in the chest. There have not been any serious attacks since then but if he stopped his medication (one third daily dosage) his chest tightened. Pain and stiffness in several joints and his lower back. He had chicken pox which was slow to heal.

Family History:
He came from a farming family with two older brothers and his parents were looking to retire which meant the farm became the property of the two older brothers. This had led to several arguments within the family over many years as this man was extremely keen to continue the farm work but his brothers would not let him have a say in the day to day running or long term future of the farm. He had recently married.

Our Findings:
The asthma attacks as a child were brought on by the family arguments. He felt he was unable to express his opinion within this family situation leading to a disruption of the throat chakra (communication and judgement). He felt a constant sense of unknowing of what his future would be as his brothers would not make any final decision as to his future role on the farm leading to a weakness within the first chakra (security) causing the lower back and joint problems. As the youngest brother he had not been taken very seriously by his brothers which had led to low self esteem. This had

weakened the fourth chakra (expression of love towards self) and the immune system (thymus gland) leading to a situation where if he suffered any illness, they were slow to heal.

The ideal situation would be for him to look for other forms of employment until the family dispute had settled and he knew where he stood as far as the farm inheritance was concerned. As this was an ongoing problem, where he had no control over the final outcome, remaining within the situation would only make his symptoms worse.

For his homework, we suggested he put his energies into another part of his life where he could exercise control. This could be something like a hobby or a sport, where these kinds of activities would help to strengthen the first chakra until the family issue was resolved. As these new activities would help boost his self esteem, they would also help with the fourth chakra and his immune system. A short course of the herb echinacea three or four times a year would also help to boost his immune system. For the lung weakness, we suggested he start with the giveaway and follow on with an activity such as singing or drama classes to help boost the fifth chakra.

Case Two
A woman in her forties.

Medical History:
There had been steady weight gain which had become excessive in the past three years (45 lbs - 20 kg) despite following a strict diet. Thyroid problems were suspected but not medically confirmed. Feeling very tired with occasional anxiety attacks. Asthma type chest problems. A feeling of non-existence.

Personal History:
Married for twenty years to a successful and ambitious businessman who was also an extreme hypochondriac. He was being treated for an assumed serious illness for a long period of time which turned out to be only a minor problem.

Our Findings:
Weight gain of this nature usually only occurs for one of two reasons, or as in this case, for both reasons. The spleen (third chakra, personal power and emotions - the spleen specifically deals with frustration) controls the lower body lymph tissue and frustration tends to block this function of the spleen which always leads to weight gain. If you have gained weight and a diet has not helped, think how much frustration there is in your life - if you can clear the frustration, the weight will disappear automatically without dieting. In this woman's case, there had been extreme frustration at her husband's condition and the final medical diagnosis of his condition not being serious coincided with the start of her rapid weight gain.

The other reason for weight gain is the thyroid. The thyroid links in to the fifth chakra (communication and judgement) specifically into a sense of being blocked from saying what you think. In this case, the woman had felt unable to say what she thought as her husband's assumed condition was potentially life threatening and she did not wish to add to his problems by saying what was on her mind. The same chakra controls the lungs and her asthma type symptoms arose for the same reasons (not getting her thoughts off her chest). The thyroid problem also gave rise to her other symptoms. In this case, the thyroid became under active and, in chakra terms, that would read as someone who wished to bury themselves away by puffing themselves up to look bigger than they felt inside.

Essentially, this woman had buried herself away in order to look after her husband. When she realised that he was not as ill as he had made out, all of her pent up emotions broke loose and the chakras associated with those emotions reacted strongly bringing about the physical symptoms.

The chakras are a direct link to the soul. All that the soul asks is that we bring balance to our lives. If we go too far in one direction, as with this woman, the chakras become depleted and the consciousness will respond by letting the body know, in no uncertain terms, that it is not amused.

Our homework suggestion was the giveaway (we do not condone domestic violence - even if he might deserve it!) and for her to look for a life outside of the home as there was no longer any reason for her to spend most of her time looking after her husband.

Whilst the giveaway is extremely effective in clearing the spleen of its accumulated frustration, the lymphatic system is extremely extensive and can sometimes, as in this case, become severely blocked. To clear these kinds of blockages would take several hours of healing work whereas there are other approaches which can help to soften and clear lymphatic tissue and so we recommended a course of lymph drainage massages and/or a visit to a herbalist for advice on herbal tinctures to help soften and clear the lymph tissue. We also suggested taking up singing classes or even singing along to the radio or tape in her car as these kinds of activities would give her more confidence in using her voice as well as help to put energy back into the fifth chakra.

Case Three
A woman in her late fifties.

Medical History:
Diagnosed as having Crohn's Disease 20 years ago although the symptoms were quite vague. They included stomach pains and a sense of bloating in the abdomen, mucus in the stools,

raging diarrhoea at times and strong colicky pains after eating, a feeling of no energy and a lack of concentration. She had undergone a partial hysterectomy a couple of years ago and there was a diagnosis of an ovarian cyst.

Family History:
There had been a history of conflict between her and her husband resulting in a divorce a number of years ago. Her sons still lived at home and were demanding and inconsiderate. Her ex husband was still involved with the family and tended to cause trouble occasionally.

Our Findings:
In our experience, Crohn's Disease is caused by the spleen controlled lymph tissue becoming blocked over a prolonged period (third chakra - the spleen relates specifically to frustration). This has the affect of the lymph nodes becoming very swollen and distorting the intestines (the underlying cause for diverticulitis). The intestines are all about, on a chakra level, emotional "debris" that we have been hanging onto for a prolonged period which has the affect of slowing down the digestive system. The two conditions together, a slow digestion and prolonged frustration, generates Crohn's Disease. In chakra terms, this reads as long term frustration at holding onto old emotions.

The spleen also feeds various vitamins into the stomach to keep it moist and functioning smoothly, if this function is affected it can result in the colicky pains described by this woman after eating. The chakra reading of this would be frustration at having to "swallow" herself over a prolonged period. With her digestion being so disrupted, it was not surprising that she felt a lack of energy and her concentration was suffering because of it. On another level, by remaining within the situation with her ex husband, accepting her lack of response to the situation for a long time, her pancreas had become affected (third chakra - emotional force). The pancreas produces a hormone called somatostatin which regulates the activity within the brain. With the pancreas affected on this level, her concentration also suffered.

The hysterectomy and ovarian cyst were clearly due to the ongoing problems with her ex husband (second chakra).

Our homework suggestions were basically to let go, to stop being the martyr to everyone and begin to live her life for herself. Her sons were adult and could make their own arrangements to visit their father so she did not have to put up with his visits and she could take more control over this part of her old life. A creative hobby would also help to re-energise the second chakra helping to resolve the gynaecological problems. We also suggested a concerted effort with the giveaway to clear out the intestines, spleen and pancreas (when she did get down to using the giveaway, she reported that the first time she ripped up her writing it felt like a huge weight had been lifted - something that had been held tightly just released. A change to an organic diet would help with her energy levels and clear out some of the toxins trapped within the abdominal lymphs.

Case Four
A woman in her eighties.

Medical History:
She had TB and pleurisy about forty years ago. Current x-rays show a shadow on the left lung which appeared to be a fibrous growth. Uses an inhaler and nebuliser daily. She had bad catarrh which was long and stringy. There was pain in her left shoulder and neck with a restriction in movement. She lost weight a little while ago and has been unable to regain it. A barium x-ray showed possible diverticulitis. She also had tinnitus in her left ear.

Family History:
She had been married to a man for sixty years who, especially since retiring, had become less and less active and unwilling to do anything for himself. An old fashioned woman who was brought up to believe that she has to do everything around the home and look after her husband.

Our Findings:
Her symptoms are fairly typical of women of her generation.
The lung problems (fifth chakra - self expression) stem from her seeing herself as the home maker and women of her generation were not allowed to express their thoughts - literally not able to get anything off her chest, leading to severe congestion and various illnesses.

The neck, shoulder and tinnitus all arose because of the thymus being blocked (fourth chakra - expression of love towards self). The upper body lymph tissue is controlled by the thymus and fourth chakra problems of this nature always tend to block up the lymph tissue leading to the muscles in her shoulder and neck becoming stiff. The lymph tissues drain unwanted toxins out of the muscles and other tissues and if the lymphs become blocked up because of the thymus problem, the muscles can become very stiff.

Her tinnitus arose for the same reason. In our experience, most cases of tinnitus are blocked lymph tissue in the neck pushing the main artery in the neck against the back of the ear. The sounds heard by tinnitus sufferers can be the sound of their own blood rushing through the artery amplified by the inner ear.

On a chakra level, both of these conditions also relate to her husband's attitude since he retired. The shoulder problem would arise because she was now "shouldering" too much responsibility in her life and the tinnitus was a sign that she did not want to listen to what her husband had to say.

The intestinal problems really stem from the same sort of situations - a lifetime of not being herself but subservient to her husband and her children, leading to a holding in of all her emotions and personal power.

Our homework suggestions were to start with the giveaway to help clear both third and fifth chakras. After sixty years of living in one particular way it is very difficult to change habits, however it is possible to learn some new ones. As her husband did not want to take part in any social activity and her children had left home, we suggested that she began to look at adult education classes to begin investigating who she was - something she had never done before. Alternatively, she could begin voluntary work for a charity as this would take her out of the home and begin working with other people or animals as this would raise her self image (fourth chakra) and increase her sense of self (third chakra - personal power). An occasional aromatherapy massage would also be beneficial as this would give her a treat also helping the fourth chakra.

Case Five
A man in his forties.

Medical History:
About seven months previously a disc had prolapsed in the lower back putting pressure onto the sciatic nerve serving the left leg. He was seeing an osteopath who had put the disc back into place several times but it kept moving out of place. An x-ray suggested that there was the beginning of osteoarthritis in the region. There was constant pain to the left hip and left leg. The medical advice was to stay in bed on his back for a month and take anti-inflammatory drugs which he did not consider to be a suitable course of action.

Family History:
He was a single man, divorced several years previously. His work was highly stressed and he had recently suffered a

major setback in his promotion prospects leading to him feeling very insecure as to his position within the company.

Our Findings:
A classic case of first chakra insecurity problems manifesting in the two regions of his life which were causing him the most problems.The sciatic nerve leaves the spinal cord in a position just below the third chakra (personal power). The problems experienced at his work gave him a very strong insecurity about his position (personal power) which had led to a slippage of the spine at the third chakra position. There had been a minor problem with his hip prior to the sciatic nerve movement brought about by his divorce (second chakra insecurity usually manifests itself in the hip joint) and the third chakra movement had aggravated the problem.

To help prevent these problems from re-occurring, we suggested that if it was not possible to resolve his position at work that he take up self assertiveness classes to help boost his self esteem to help "ground" the energies of the first chakra. The classes would also help strengthen the third chakra.

Case Six
A woman in her thirties.

Medical History:
She has had sciatic pain for a number of years which is with her for 90% of the time. There is a diagnosis of Irritable Bowel Syndrome (IBS). Constant pain in both the lower and upper back. Her prescribed painkillers only made the stomach condition worse and physiotherapy had not made any difference. The x-rays that had been taken were inconclusive as were the blood tests.

Family History:
This was a woman whose husband tended to stray into affairs occasionally. She was confident within herself but felt insecure within the marriage.

Our Findings:
Her problems stemmed from the insecurity she felt within her marriage. The pressure on the sciatic nerve was as a result of one of her hips being displaced. Hip problems almost always arise from some form of insecurity within a relationship (second chakra). With the hip being unstable, it tends to put a reverse curve into the spine. In this case the reverse curve concentrated pressure in the region between the shoulder blades. This was further aggravated by the fourth chakra (how love is expressed) being depleted as she was not sure how her expressions of love towards her husband were being received, creating a further weakness in the spine at this point (between the shoulder blades). The nerves that control the function of the stomach leave the spine at this point and any spinal displacement in this area will fool the brain into telling the stomach to produce a constant supply of digestive acids. Too much acid aggravates the stomach leading to her diagnosis of IBS.

On a chakra basis, her symptoms can be read as insecurity within her marriage (hip) and insecurity within how she expressed her love (between the shoulder blades) and being within a situation which she could not stomach. This is how seemingly unrelated symptoms can be linked together to provide a full story of someone's life.

The only realistic way of approaching this kind of problem (relationship problems can be difficult to resolve especially where there are practical problems surrounding one partner leaving) is to work with the second chakra on its primary function - creativity. We suggested that she make more use of her creative skills as this would strengthen the second chakra which would help to keep the hips and spine stronger in the future and prevent the return of the pressure on the sciatic nerve and the nerves to the stomach.

Case Seven

A woman in her forties.

Medical History:
There was severe psoriasis to the lower legs that had been there for twenty years. She had tried a number of approaches to try to alleviate the problem but all had ultimately failed. She also suffered from strong headaches which she had had since a child. She also had a constant battle with gaining too much weight.

Family History:
Her natural mother had died of liver cancer when she was very young and had been brought up by a step mother with whom she had extreme difficulty in all aspects of their relationship. She had left home as soon as she could and her psoriasis had begun at that time. Her relationship with her father was quite amicable but there were continuing problems with her step mother.As her mother had died of liver cancer, she was terrified that she was going to die of the same problem and saw her psoriasis as an indicator of liver problems.

As a note about inherited illnesses. It is a common belief that a tendency towards illnesses such as cancer are inherited from our parents. In our experience, this is not the case. In virtually all instances, the only inherited factor in illness is a learned pattern of behaviour. Parents pass onto their children a way of approaching life and if that approach goes against the wishes of the soul, a straying from the ideal balance of life, the same illness will develop in different people but for the same reasons, giving the appearance of a genetic defect.

In this instance, if the daughter becomes her own person, the incorrect forms of behaviour that led to illness for the mother will not occur with the daughter. This case is a prime example of how the process works. The liver is controlled by the third chakra (personal power and emotions) but specifically deals with the emotions of fear, jealousy and guilt. The state of constant fear of liver problems in this woman mirrors a learnt behaviour from her childhood so unless the pattern of thought was broken, liver cancer could actually follow.

Our Findings:
To start with the headaches. As a child, she was denied any love and not allowed to express her love to others as it was rejected by her stepmother. She was also prevented from honouring (loving) herself as her stepmother constantly put her down. This situation led to the thymus (fourth chakra) becoming blocked and the upper body lymph system putting pressure onto the muscles and nerves of the skull resulting in headaches.

The psoriasis was caused by a similar problem. The liver function was actually quite good despite the years of fear and guilt, however, the spleen function was severely disrupted because of the years of frustration with her father and step mother. The psoriasis was caused by the lower body lymph system (third chakra) being totally blocked and the only way in which the lymphs could drain was through the skin. The skin will become affected where there is a sense of insecurity (first chakra) relating to the fact that she felt she needed some help in resolving her problems. The skin will be affected in situations where the person affected is saying "I am feeling insecure and I am letting you know that I would like some help and reassurance".

The weight gain was also caused by the blocked lower body lymph tissue. This is why her dieting never worked, if the emotions are locked into place, excess weight will never be lost.

Our suggestions to her were these. Use the giveaway. There were years of locked in emotions which needed to be cleared, particularly the frustration locked up in the spleen. With the spleen clear of its accumulated frustration, the lymphs would be free to drain properly clearing the psoriasis. To assist in releasing these problems, we also suggested a full body lymph drainage massage. This type of massage can be quite painful but they are well worth it. To help illustrate the point, we know of someone who, following a lymph massage, lost two inches off her waistline! (she put it all back on again as she had not dealt with the underlying frustrations in her life - the giveaway is needed to make the massage effective over a period of time).

To help with the thymus and upper body lymph problem we suggested that she begin a regime where she spent a certain amount of time just for herself. This involved such things as buying herself a bunch of flowers, a bar of organic chocolate, a glass of her favourite tipple, beginning to look at the things she had always wanted to do but had always found excuses not to. Really, to begin a new relationship with herself where she could say "I am worth being spoilt" - it works wonders for these kinds of problems. Incidentally, if you are worried about the chocolate suggestion, see chapter twelve for the reasons why they are not the bad guys you thought they were.

Case Eight
A man in his forties.

Medical History:
A long history of Raynaud's disease (lack of blood circulation to the extremities) to the feet. There were spinal problems to

the lower right back and to the neck. Irritable Bowel Syndrome (IBS) for a number of years with excessive flatulence with a tendency for internal cramps. A long history of very fitful sleep.

Family History:
A single man who had difficulty finding his sexuality, he felt that he was gay but could not quite resolve the issue. He had been unemployed for a long time and had difficulty coming to terms with this situation.

Our Findings:
The back and neck problems really came from a combination of the first and second chakras. The first chakra (security) had been disrupted over a prolonged period by a combination of the unemployment and the sexuality issue which put a general weakness into the whole spinal structure. Because of the sexuality issue, the spine/pelvis joint had been weakened putting a slight "wobble" in the pelvis at the sacro/illiac joint (second chakra). This had a tendency to put the spine into a slightly reverse curve which manifested itself at the neck.

The IBS came from a combination of problems all associated with the third chakra (personal power and emotions). The sexuality issue brought about a large emotional conflict which was contributed to by the long term unemployment. The liver (fear) was affected and its blood cleansing function was slowed contributing to the Reynaud's. The gall bladder (anger - mainly at himself for not being able to resolve his issues) was slowing down his digestion and was responsible for the flatulence. The spleen (frustration) was blocking the functioning of the lower body, especially abdominal lymphatic system which was responsible for the abdominal cramps. The pancreas (emotional force) was slowing down the digestion process by not producing sufficient digestive enzymes and, very importantly, the fitful sleep came from the over production of a pancreatic hormone (called somatostatin) which controls the activity in the synaptic gaps in the brain. The reason for this problem is that as he could not resolve his sexuality issue, the consciousness stimulated this hormone to keep him awake until he did make some kind of resolution.

The Raynaud's disease is a fourth chakra problem. The body can be very literal at times and this condition is a perfect example. The fourth chakra is all about how we express our love and controls the heart and blood circulation. By being afraid to step into a new way of expressing his love, he slowed down the circulation of the blood. He literally had cold feet about his sexuality.

Our suggestions to him were to join self assertive classes to help him to gain confidence in himself and what he had to offer the world (first, third and fourth chakras). Until he could satisfactorily resolve his sexuality issues, we suggested that he take up a creative pastime as energy put into a chakra's primary function (the second chakra's primary function is creativity) can override problems with the chakra's secondary function (sexual relationships).

Case Nine
A woman in her late sixties.

Medical History:
There had been a large cancerous mass around the ovaries and uterus which had been surgically removed two years ago. Since then, the abdominal walls had collapsed causing a partial prolapse to the bladder and the vagina. There was an arthritis type problem with the right knee. There had been a history of lower back problems which had resulted in the collapse of one of the discs for which surgery had been performed (laminectomy). There was a sense of "fizzing" in the muscles of the neck and shoulders which had been diagnosed as osteoporosis. There was also osteoporosis of the lower back.

Family History:
Her first marriage had ended forty years previously and it had been disastrous. Her second marriage was one of companionship but there was very little in the way of expressions of love, either physical or emotional, since the birth of her two children over thirty years ago.

Our Findings:
On a chakra basis, the first, second, third and fourth chakras were very depleted.The first chakra is connected with the skeleton, the joints and the bladder. The second chakra is connected with the reproductive system. The third chakra is connected with all of the abdominal organs and the fourth chakra is connected with the immune and endocrine (hormone) systems.

Her first marriage had generated an underlying weakness within the first chakra (sense of security) and the second chakra (sexual relationships). Whilst her second marriage was very close and companionable, it did not fulfil her need for stronger expressions of love and this led to her still feeling a little insecure, holding the weakness within the first chakra. The lack of sufficient nurturing, and sex, within her second marriage also held the problems with the second chakra in place.

The back problem is located in the region of the second chakra reflecting her sense of insecurity within her relationships with both husbands. This is further demonstrated by the cancer to the reproductive organs.

The knee problem stems from a general sense of insecurity (instability) within most regions of her life as she felt that her marriage did not fulfil or support her emotional and sexual needs. This lack of support also generated a lack of self worth which affected the fourth chakra, especially relating to the thymus gland. The thymus gland controls the function of the upper body lymphatic system and the lack of self worth was causing this to block, backing up the lymph tissue to the neck and shoulders causing the feelings of "fizzing".

This sounds quite complicated, but if you break the problems down to their chakra components, they become simpler to understand.Spine and knee problems are connected to the first chakra which relates to our sense of security. The spinal problem was located in the lower back, close to where the second chakra is located and reflected her insecurity within her marriage. The cancer was located within the second chakra organs also reflecting the problems within her relationships.The neck and shoulder problems are a little more difficult to track down. Muscular problems are also related to the first chakra and where the muscles are sore or painful, it is likely to be a sense of insecurity causing the problem. However, the description here was of a fizzing and the most likely cause of this feeling will be a blockage in the lymph tissue and, as we are talking of the upper body, it must relate to the thymus gland (fourth chakra - self honouring).

Our homework suggestion to her was to take up a creative hobby, preferably one where she shared it with other people. The creative side will help to balance the second chakra and overcome her continuing relationship problems, it would also help with her sense of self worth as she would be able to see that she was capable of creating something of value. Doing something practical would help with her insecurity issues as would the social interaction with other class members.

To prevent the return of the osteoporosis, we suggested that she include more organic green, leafy vegetables in her diet. All green leafy vegetables contain high levels of calcium in a form which the body finds easy to absorb. Most calcium supplements are not easily absorbed by the body and can cause problems with stones in the kidneys as the body flushes a high percentage of this form of calcium away. Most dairy products also generate similar problems for similar reasons. Another way of helping bone calcium mass is to take gentle exercise as often as possible. The easiest and best form of exercise is walking. In this woman's case, joining a rambling group would help on several levels - bone mass and social interaction.

Chapter Four

Not So Straightforward Cases

In chapter three, we looked at some case histories that we would consider to be fairly straight forward. In this chapter, we will be looking at some cases that are a little more complex.

Case Ten
A woman in her thirties.

Medical History:
Poor quality sleep for many years which made her feel depressed. She was a bit of a worrier and things tended to go round and round in her head. Several years ago there were ME type problems which had not fully cleared. Five years ago she was diagnosed as having severe endometriosis (inflammation of the uterus lining) which resulted in a partial hysterectomy. IBS (Irritable Bowel Syndrome) type problems for several years which were also complicated by bowel cysts although this condition was beginning to improve. There was a need to urinate quite frequently. Quite bad sinus problems for a number of years following a bout of glandular fever. She was quite skinny and found great difficulty in putting on weight. There was lower back pain.

Personal History:
She had met and married her husband whilst she was still in the throes of her ME and had realised that their relationship was not really the basis for a successful marriage so she was in the process of separation and divorce. Her relationship with her parents had not been good and there were continuing problems with them. She had been unable to decide on a suitable career and so tended to drift from job to job. She was quite psychic but had not pursued this side of her life.

Our Findings:
First chakra: this chakra was very weak due to her not having a settled home life since childhood. This had put a weakness into the whole spine and the kidney and adrenal glands were underfunctioning leading to some hormone problems and the frequent urination.

Second Chakra: the problems with her marriage led to her reducing her want to nurture. This removal of this part of her nature brought about the endometriosis and the lack of security within her marriage brought about the lower back pain.

Third chakra: her gall bladder (suppressed anger) tended to block and clear leading to a cycle of diarrhoea and constipation, this was further added to by her spleen (frustration) not feeding the correct vitamins into the stomach which made the stomach dry and "tight". Her pancreas (the force used in expressing our emotions) was dysfunctional on two levels. The first was that it was not feeding digestive enzymes into her digestive system very well, leading to difficulties in breaking down food. The second is to do with a pancreatic hormone (somatostatin) which controls the level of activity in the brain. As she rarely resolved any problems, this hormone was over stimulated resulting in her sleeplessness (her consciousness would not let her sleep until she resolved something).

Fourth chakra: there was a breakdown in the endocrine system (the body's hormonal balance) brought about by the chakra's primary function (the link between the consciousness and the physical body). The secondary function was also disrupted (expressions of love) through the thymus gland (self love) which had led to the original glandular problems and was responsible for the continuing sinus trouble - blocked lymphs again!

Fifth chakra: the lungs (self expression of thoughts) were not very efficient at oxygenating the blood leading to a sense of weariness. The thyroid (prevented from speaking thoughts) was heavily over functioning (hyperactive) leading to the weight loss problems. On a chakra basis, this would read as someone who wants to make themselves look smaller, disappear so that no one would ask her opinion - especially her husband.

Sixth chakra: the pituitary gland - the body's main hormone control gland (links in with the chakra's primary function of psychic vision) was not functioning very well which was further adding to the hormone imbalance.

Seventh chakra: the pineal gland was over producing melatonin (the hormone that makes us sleep and the cause of true ME) so there was a sense of constant tiredness. This was left over from her ME as she had not resolved all of the issues surrounding the illness. The pineal is directly linked into the higher self and problems with this gland are because we have gone against the direction the soul wishes us to.

Basically, her system was in complete conflict. The thyroid problems tried to make her hyperactive yet the pineal gland tried to make her sleep. This was further complicated by the pancreatic hormone keeping her awake.

It appears to be quite a mess and immensely complicated but, if you begin to break the symptoms down on a chakra basis, it becomes easier to understand. Essentially, this is a woman who has drifted through her life and not taken any steps in a positive direction. The ME is indicative that, on a higher level, she was going in the wrong direction. The marriage she took on whilst suffering from the ME was also something which was not the right thing to do. All of the other symptoms are as a direct result of these first two actions.

Fortunately, she was taking corrective actions by the time she came to see us by arranging the separation from her husband, finding her own home (to give herself greater security) and taking a very close look at all of the other areas in her life and making major changes.

If she found that she still could not sleep at night, we suggested that she begin to write down the thoughts that were going through her head. This would help to clarify the thoughts for her and she would be more able to see the regions of her life which still needed some assistance and clearance.

Another technique which is quite useful in these kinds of instances is to use a different form of writing exercise. This involves writing two lists. The first is made up of all of the activities that you currently spend your time doing, both day and night. This should include all of the activities that make up your day and every day. The second list should be made up of the activities that you would love to be doing. This can be as wild as you care to think, trips to Mars or around the universe are perfectly acceptable as long as you include ideas that are a little more practicable in being able to achieve them. What are your dreams? What are your innermost desires? What would you like to be doing in an ideal world? Put them onto this list - this helps to clarify your thoughts and help you realise what is really missing from your life.

Next, compare the two lists and see what you can throw out from the first to allow time to bring in activities from the second. Now that you have carried out this exercise, what is stopping you?

Case Eleven
A boy aged nine.

Medical History:
Damage to the middle of the back resulting in difficulty in walking. Hyperactive for most of the time and severely disruptive within the family. The rest of the time he is severely withdrawn - a condition known as hyper autism. He has several food allergies especially wheat (gluten) and milk.

Family History:
He is the middle child of three children. He was considered normal at birth but had developed these symptoms over the past few years and was progressively becoming worse.

Our Findings:
The key to this condition is with the fact that this boy is the middle child although this condition can arise in any child where there is more than one child in the family. It is all to do with the third chakra, personal power. Usually at birth, children such as these are considered normal, however, as they grow older they have to begin fighting for parental attention against the older child but especially the new, younger one. If they feel as though they are not receiving enough attention, they have to begin making more noise than the others (hyperactive) or they give up the fight and withdraw into themselves (autism).

The organ most affected by these situations is the pancreas, the amount of emotional force used in expressing themselves. The pancreas produces several important substances used by the body but in these cases there are two which play the greatest role. The first is a hormone called somatostatin which controls the activity that takes place within the synaptic gaps of the brain. Too much of this hormone is produced when the child does not feel as though they are receiving enough attention (hyperactive) and too little is produced if the child withdraws (autism). The second substance is digestive enzymes. These break down carbohydrates, proteins and fats into simpler substances that the body can more readily absorb. If these enzymes are not produced properly, it can result in diarrhoea and a seeming intolerance to certain foods, especially those containing gluten. This is the primary cause of food allergies or intolerances.

We suggested to his parents that they begin to look at how they interact with their children. If they were giving one child less attention than the others, to try to redress the problem by giving equal attention to all of their children and encourage the one with the problems to understand the needs of the others. The problem child could also be encouraged to make use of the giveaway, either written or painted, to express his feelings about the situation and help him to release some of the problem emotions.

The Bach Flower Remedies can be extremely helpful in these situations. In this case we recommended Holly for his jealousy and Chicory for the hyperactive aspect. There are a number of other Flower Remedies for children in these kinds of situations. The ones given here were for this specific child in his specific circumstances, other Flower Remedies for other children need to be assessed on an individual basis.

We have passed on our findings of the link between the pancreas and hyperactivity or autism in children to members of the medical profession and have not received any interest.

Case Twelve
A woman in her forties.

Medical History:
She had been feeling pain in her pelvis and hip since the birth of her first child sixteen years previously. Twelve years ago the right hip began to click, the medical diagnosis was a spina bifida type problem. Since then she has developed pain in the lower back, sharp groin pain, pain in both knees and her right ankle. She also cries spontaneously for no apparent reason.

Family History:
There were marital problems around the time of the birth of her first child and the marriage has remained a little unsteady since.

Our Findings:
The pelvis and lower back problems are very typical with women following childbirth. If these kinds of problems are not corrected following birth, they will usually result in the woman needing a hip replacement operation in later years. When a woman becomes pregnant, the bones of the pelvis (illiac bones) gradually hinge on the joint between the illiac and the sacrum bones to allow more room in the pelvic cavity for the growth of the fetus. After giving birth, these three bones should resume their correct position. In this case, the sacro/illiac joint (second chakra) had not returned to its correct position (there was a slippage to the right side of the joint) making the sacrum and coccyx bones move position. This movement slackened the tension in the cartilage that stretches from the sacrum and holds the femur (thigh bone) in place. Over the years, the femur became loose and started to wear away the end of the femur and the hip socket. The resulting tilt in the pelvis also put increased pressure onto the knees and the ankles. This added pressure would normally be tolerated by these joints but as she was feeling fairly unstable within her life (first chakra), the joints began to give way.

The spontaneous crying was a little unusual but stemmed from a fourth chakra disruption. As is common with most women, the thymus and lymph tissue were badly blocked (expressing love towards the self) and the blockage was putting pressure behind the eyes, making them weep. Given her emotional state, once the eyes began to weep, it would trigger an emotional response as well and she would cry.

As her sense of security (first chakra) and her relationship problems (second chakra) were the main issues, we suggested she return to the creative career she gave up for her husband. This was met with a great deal of enthusiasm as she had always missed this side of her life. If it is not possible to walk away from an unhappy relationship, the only way to resolve these kinds of second chakra problems is with a creative pursuit of some kind which also tends to help with a greater sense of security (first chakra) and self worth (fourth chakra).

Case Thirteen
A man in his fifties.

Medical History:
He was diagnosed as having Multiple Sclerosis twenty years ago. Initially the disease was slow to progress but was now accelerating.

Family History:
He had been a very successful businessman with a wife and young family. However, he spent too much time with his business and his wife left, taking the children with her. Since his diagnosis he had not left his home and had a full time carer.

Our Findings:
The illness had begun with a loss of function of the legs and then slowly progressed up the body to a point where it was

now beginning to affect his arms and brain functions. His children rarely visited him but, when they did, his illness would worsen when they left.

On a chakra level, we are looking at the seventh chakra. His wife and family leaving him was such a shock to his system that he began to shut himself down. His realisation that it was his behaviour that led to their leaving only made the situation worse and led to a more rapid progression of his illness. Essentially, he could not cope with the loss of his wife and family and the part he had played in their leaving so he began to shut down his body, a progressive withdrawal from the outside world and into a new world of his own making.

As this is a seventh chakra problem, we are looking at a break down of the link between the soul and his conscious mind. The only way of resolving such issues is to ask the question - do I wish to stay on the planet? If the answer is yes, the symptoms can be reversed. If the answer is no - the symptoms will gradually progress with inevitable consequences. No illness is irreversible if there is a will for change.

Case Fourteen
A woman in her seventies.

Medical History:
About two and one half years ago she had developed an itching to the rectum which had gradually progressed upwards into the end of the colon. There was constant pain and itching and a steady discharge. Her doctors were baffled as to the nature of the problem and it did not respond to any treatment.

Family History:
She had had a very close loving marriage for over forty years until her husband's death about seven years ago. She had

remarried four years ago mainly for companionship and affection.

Our Findings:
Here was a very warm and loving woman who had remarried in order to find some companionship and someone to whom she could show her affection. Her new husband, however, wanted a more physical relationship than she did. Every time she cuddled up to her new husband, he thought she wanted sex but she did not, or at least not as often as he did. As soon as the itching problem began, he stopped suggesting sex and became more affectionate and supportive towards her but he had gradually withdrawn and she no longer received any kind of affection.

Really, what she had done was to create a chastity belt. As she only wanted affection rather than sex, her body responded by generating a condition which brought about her wishes. It just goes to show how powerful the mind can be and how the body will bring about the situations we want.

Our first question to her was did she actually want us to heal the problem? If we took the itching away, she would be back to square one as far as her husband and his sex drive was concerned. Our suggestion to her was to speak with her husband honestly about her thoughts and wants and try to come to a more amicable arrangement about the physical side of their relationship, she could then unlock the chastity belt by herself.

Case Fifteen
A woman in her thirties.

Medical History:
She had been trying to start a family for eleven years without success. She had had two IVF (In Vetro Fertilization -

artificial insemination) treatments which had been unsuccessful. There had been a blockage to one of the fallopian tubes which had been surgically cleared.

Family History:
Her husband was very keen on having children but she was undecided as she was interested in pursuing her career. The IVF treatments had been tried in order to fulfil her husband's wishes.

Our Findings:
A very clear case of a second chakra problem where there is a conflict between family and career. By being undecided about whether she wanted a family or a career, her body had responded by putting her reproductive capability onto hold until she made her final decision. Once she made a clear decision one way or the other, her body would react accordingly. If she made a clear commitment to having a child because she wanted one, as opposed to responding to her husband's wishes for a child, her body would respond, resulting in a natural pregnancy.

Incidentally, we also found that the chemical residue from the IVF drugs was actively preventing a normal pregnancy occurring as it made the uterus lining too soft to accept a natural single egg implant.

Case Sixteen
A woman in her thirties.

Medical History:
There was a history of lumps in her breasts since puberty and she began to feel a lump in her breast about three months ago which had gradually hardened. She had very recently had a diagnosis of breast cancer confirmed. Her periods were irregular and very heavy. There had been a history of ME type

problems which had never fully cleared. There was constant pain in her upper back and neck.

Family History:
She had married a domineering husband of whom her young child was petrified. She was in the process of leaving her husband. Both her mother and sister had breast cancer from which her mother had recently died.

Our Findings:
The period problems were clearly second chakra problems with her husband. The rest of her problems also stemmed from the same root cause. As mentioned previously, illnesses run in families because of learned behaviour passed from parent to child, in this case mother to both daughters, all of whom had married domineering men. As they were so dominated, they were unable to see themselves as individuals in their own right and their self esteem suffered as a result (fourth chakra).

The cancer is the ultimate result of the blockages to the thymus gland (fourth chakra) and the upper body lymphatic tissue. Virtually all breast cancers are caused in this way.

In this woman's case, there were three lymph nodes in the breast which had become cancerous. However, her decision and initial steps to leave her husband, had actually switched off the cancer growth and the hard lump she felt was no longer actively cancerous. The breast lump problem had also been aggravated by the fact that she was extremely fit and active and wore an extremely tight bra for sports activities all day and every day, preventing the free flow of the lymph fluids.

By learning the behaviour patterns of her mother, she had followed her example and married a man who was as domineering as her father which, on a soul level, was a very wrong direction to take and the ME resulted (seventh chakra).

The back and neck problems came about from an insecurity (first chakra putting a weakness into the whole spine) manifesting itself in the region of the fourth chakra (between the shoulder blades) reflecting her insecurity about how she could express her love to her husband and, more importantly, to herself.

Although she realised that the cancer was no longer active, she decided to proceed with surgery as the cutting out of the lump represented, to her, the cutting out of the problem from her life. With the lump gone, she felt she really had started her new life. By bringing about a number of changes within her life, she had acknowledged herself as a person in her own right and deserving of a greater love than she had received from her husband. This change of thought, and the other actions she had taken, would prevent the cancer problem from returning. These changes in her life also gave her a greater sense of security (first chakra), preventing the back problems from returning. Her bra also went into the bin!

The comment about the bra is very serious. Any bra will prevent the free flow of fluid around the lymphatic system so it is important to find as many times as possible where you can remove your bra and let your system function more efficiently.

Case Seventeen
A man in his eighties.

Medical History:
There had been a progressive loss of vision over the past seven or eight years resulting in a blurring of vision in the centre of both eyes with the right eye being worse than the

left. His peripheral vision was unaffected. The medical diagnosis was of macular degeneration (a breakdown of the light receptors in the back of the eye by fluid leaking from the inner eye). He also had to urinate frequently.

Family History:
He had lived a very active outdoor life all of his life which had stopped when he had retired. His wife of over fifty years had died about ten years ago. He spent most of his time indoors by himself.

Our Findings:
The urinary problem stems from the link between the first chakra and the kidneys. As this man had lived on his own for a number of years, he had become increasingly less confident and this usually leads to a weakness within the first chakra affecting the kidneys (the main cause of incontinence in both the young and the elderly).

The eye sight problems have a similar basis. The left eye links into the sixth chakra (physical senses and psychic vision) whilst the right eye links into the seventh chakra (the link to the higher elements of our consciousness). Since retiring and his wife passing away, there had been a progressive loss of vision in the right eye as he slowly withdrew himself from his life's purpose disrupting the link with the soul. The same applied to the left eye as he could literally see no future for himself. Essentially, a withdrawing from the world as he could not see his life continuing in any meaningful way.

The only way of resolving problems such as these is to find a new interest in life, a new focus of attention to give his life a new purpose and, quite literally in this case, something to look forward to.

Chapter Five

Even Less Straightforward Cases

Case Eighteen
A woman in her twenties

Medical History:
This was a young woman who had been diagnosed as having multiple sclerosis about twelve years ago. There were a very large number of symptoms all painful and consistent with a gradual breaking down of the central nervous system. She had urinary frequency problems and the centre of her eyes were becoming misty.

Family History:
Up until the death of her parents fifteen years previously she had been perfectly healthy. Her older sister saw their parents death as an opportunity to take over this woman's life. As she gradually succumbed to her sister's dominance, there was a gradual onset of the symptoms.

Our Findings:
On a chakra level we are looking at the primary functions of the fourth and seventh chakras. The fourth is the link between the higher self and the physical body and the giving over of herself in this way led to the breakdown of the endocrine system (the body's hormonal balance). The seventh chakra is the direct link into the higher self or soul on a

primary energy link level. Giving herself over to her sister in this way led to a breakdown of this link and the higher elements of her central nervous system began to break down leading to the gradual disintegration of the nerve tissue within the body. The domineering sister had done such a good job on persuading this woman that she should take over all aspects of her life that she had literally given her whole self over to the sister on every level.

The urinary problems link into the first chakra and relates to her soul attempting to clear this problem, her sister, out of her system.

The eye problem represents her refusal to look at what was happening to her. She literally did not want to see what was in front of her face.

By helping her to understand the root causes of her problem, this woman had begun to realise that her sister was too much in control and began to take back certain aspects of her life. As she began this process, her symptoms started to diminish. The more she continued to regain control of her life, the better she became.

Case Nineteen
A man in his seventies.

Medical History:
About six months previously, he had developed a boil behind his ear which grew over two weeks to the size of an egg. The growth was surgically removed and the biopsy taken showed that it was cancerous. There was frequent urination with the painful passing of a large number of stones. There was glaucoma in one eye and constant tinnitus in both ears. He also had a fairly constant aching in his shoulders.

Family History:
He was a retired successful businessman who had lived alone for all of his life. He had been in the Navy in the second world war and the experience had traumatised him to a point where he had never fully recovered. A very gentle man.

Our Findings:
There were very strong problems on every level.

First chakra: he had a recurring sense of insecurity which he saw as an ongoing problem. This affected the kidneys rather than the spine as the kidneys represent recurring insecurities rather than a constant one. The urinary problems were added to by a third chakra problem.

Second chakra: having spent his whole life alone and celibate, he had totally blocked the function of this chakra. This led to prostate problems in particular and many of the stones he passed were solidified seminal fluid.

Third chakra: his living alone and, particularly, his war memories, led to a constant sense of guilt and fear which was having a major effect on his liver leading to blood cleansing problems. He had a very strong sense of frustration at not being able to deal with the war memories which was affecting his spleen. This meant that the spleen could not clear the lower body lymph tissue and, together with the drop in liver function, was holding toxins within the lymphs and the blood feeding a constant supply of waste products to the kidneys leading to the formation of a large quantity of stones.

Fourth chakra: he had a much reduced sense of self worth, again mainly stemming from his war experiences and this led to the upper body lymph tissue becoming totally blocked further adding to the load on the liver and kidneys. It was the lymph tissue becoming totally blocked which had caused the cancerous growth behind his ear. His tinnitus was also caused by the lymph tissue being blocked. In our experience, most cases of tinnitus are caused by the blocked lymph tissue pressing on the main artery passing next to the ear and the sound of the tinnitus is the sound of the blood rushing through the artery. The shoulder pains were also caused by the blocked lymphs holding toxins within the muscles (on a chakra level, he felt as though he was shouldering too much responsibility for his war experiences).

Our suggestion to him was to begin to write his autobiography to literally give away all of his experiences onto paper. Whilst he was holding these experiences and memories within his system, he was unable to function normally and all of his problems arose. By putting all of his wartime experiences onto paper, it would help him to put them into perspective and see that he did not need to feel guilt at surviving when others, who he saw as more deserving of life, did not.

We all eventually die. The method of our death is one which is usually appropriate to ourselves. The higher self brings about a set of circumstances where we pass over in a way which reflects the choices we have made. In times of war, many people offer their lives as a gift so that others might live. We tried to help him to understand that others die for their own reasons and that there should be no guilt for surviving when others did not.

For the prostate problem, we suggested that he take up a creative hobby. In this instance we felt that painting would be the most appropriate approach as he had a good eye for detail and the painting could help the giveaway process, depending upon the subject matter he chose.

We also suggested a series of lymph drainage massages as well as consulting a herbalist for lymph softening herbs and/or a homeopath for similar remedies.

Case Twenty.

A woman in her fifties.

Medical History:
She had a history of severe back problems both with the muscles and the bone structure. She had difficulty in breathing both from the pain and the restricted muscle movement. There were shooting pains into both legs and she had difficulty in moving, sitting or standing. There was severe bone loss to several places in her spine of up to 50% of the bone density.

Family History:
She had been sexually abused as a teenager by her father and her mother had insisted that she leave home as soon as possible and so she married the first man who asked her. She had never forgiven her mother for allowing the abuse to occur or then to continue. Her husband had taken her away from her home area and she had resented the move and never really recovered from it.

Our Findings:
This is a combination of first and fifth chakra problems. The events as a teenager totally depleted the first chakra from which it never really recovered. All of the following events built upon this first shock to the system keeping the chakra totally depleted. The initial denial of events by the mother effectively put a "gag" on the fifth chakra and she felt that she could not speak about the events for a number of years. This blocking on her speech affected the parathyroid (glands embedded in the thyroid which controls the body's calcium balance) and so aggravated the insecurity problem that it stripped the bones of their calcium. The role of the parathyroid is to maintain a balance of calcium in the blood and calcium in the bones, the body sees calcium in the blood as being more important than maintaining the level of calcium in the bones. With the parathyroid being so

dysfunctional, it stripped the bones of their calcium and deposited it in the blood which meant that the muscles locked solid as they could not function with so much calcium flowing in them. In this instance, the parathyroid was affected as it represented her emotionally "eating herself" away with her secret as she could not let the world know of her experiences.

The best way of dealing with problems such as these is to confront the person or persons who brought about the problem in the first place. In this case, her mother, her father and her husband. However, it is not always easy or desirable for such confrontations to occur and so, in those instances, the only realistic way of beginning to resolve problems like this one is with the giveaway. By putting all of her unexpressed thoughts and emotions down onto paper, it began a release which started to remove the problem with the parathyroid, easing many of the muscular and bone problems. In the future, she would have to learn to express her thoughts and wants as the problem could return if she did not begin to energise the fifth chakra by expressing her thoughts as they occurred. Where it was not possible to express herself in this way, she would need to make use of the giveaway as soon as possible after she had "swallowed" her thoughts.

We also suggested a series of aromatherapy type massages as a light massage could help to release the excessive calcium locked in the muscles. With the parathyroid working properly, once the calcium was released into the blood supply, the body would begin to re-use it to rebuild the bone structures.

To boost the energy of the first chakra, she would need to take up physical pursuits which brought her into contact with the earth. These could include such pastimes as walking, gardening or doing outdoor volunteer work. Physical exercise of this type also helps to increase bone density.

Case Twenty One
A woman in her forties.

Medical History:
There was a sense of some kind of "blockage" to the right side of the body. There was pain in the right ear with some kind of deposit, the right eye moved independently, the right shoulder was painful with muscle spasms in the shoulder and upper back, the right foot was very painful. The left knee cartilage was twisted causing some discomfort. Discomfort with digestion and some digestion problems. Her periods were very irregular. She had swings between feeling very hot and very cold. Her feet occasionally became very hot and swollen. She had glandular fever about ten years ago which had left her with a lump in her throat which never cleared.

Family History:
This woman and her mother had never seen eye to eye about any subject since her childhood and felt that she had been totally blocked by her mother from doing any of the things that she had wanted to. This had left her feeling unworthy and lacking in self confidence. She had great difficulty in letting people become close to her and had trouble expressing herself in a relationship.

Our Findings:
First chakra: very depleted of energy from her underlying insecurity which led to muscle tensions and some back problems. It also aggravated the lower body joints.

Second chakra: because she had difficulty in letting people become close, it led to relationship problems. When she did finally marry, she could not communicate her feelings very well to her husband and so this chakra became depleted leading to her period problems and her insecurity within the relationship had caused a hip problem making the lower joint problem much worse.

Third chakra; she had little self esteem and therefore dealt with personal power issues very badly (the chakra's primary function). There was a huge amount of unexpressed emotions locked into the intestines leading to her digestion problems. Her frustration at not being able to resolve any of her issues led to problems with the spleen and this led to the trouble with her feet swelling through the leg lymphs blocking up.

Fourth chakra: as is normal for most women, her thymus was blocked (lack of self love), backing up the lymphatic tissue in the upper body. This led to the ear problems, the eye problems, the glandular fever (infection within the lymph nodes) and stiffness within the shoulder muscles. This stiffness also led to the temperature swings as the nerve controlling temperature levels (the main body thermostat) runs across the shoulders. With her shoulder muscles being periodically in spasm, they alternately trapped and released this nerve leading to the swings in temperature.

Our suggestions to her were to use the giveaway as much as possible focusing on the issues with her mother. In other words, writing a series of letters to her mother stating all of the things she would have liked to have said but did not. Begin a course of lymph drainage massages to clear the upper and lower body lymphs. Also to take self assertiveness classes to help build up her self esteem (fourth chakra), boost her sense of personal power (third chakra) and sense of security (first chakra). As her self esteem rose, she would be more confident in expressing her wants and needs and this would help with her relationship issues.

Case Twenty Two
A woman in her forties.

Medical History:
There had been a history of cellulitis (a bacterial infection of

the skin which breaks down cell tissue) since the age of sixteen resulting in several hospital stays and a long term taking of antibiotics - the original infection began when she started taking the pill. Fifteen years ago she had a full hysterectomy. Constant constipation and there was a lump in the intestines with chronic indigestion pains in the lower chest. There was sudden tiredness with dizziness and nausea. She had heart palpitations where her hands would swell and itch. She had constant sore throats and had two nodes surgically removed from her vocal cords. There were sore patches inside her nostrils and there was vaginal dryness. She also had constant pain in the lower left hand side of the neck.

Family History:
Her father had died when she was twelve and her mother had remarried a man who was an alcoholic, violent and who sexually abused her. There had been a complete disruption to her teenage years both by her mother and by her step father. She had married at nineteen and had given birth to a disabled daughter. She divorced eight years ago and lived with her daughter. She worked in a very stressful job but very much enjoyed it.

Our Findings:
The first chakra had been disrupted for some time putting a general weakness into the muscles of the spine. Her lower back pain was caused by kidney damage - the underlying weakness was brought about by the disruption to the chakra but it was made considerably worse by the long term use of penicillin and a blood anti-clotting drug.

The second chakra had first become disrupted because of the abuse from her step father in her teenage years. This kind of abuse can cause a great deal of confusion to the person and disruption to the chakra, resulting in the hysterectomy. Starting on the pill at an early age also caused severe hormonal problems because of the second chakra problems which led partly to the cellulitis occurring. Skin cells contain oestrogen receptors and her system being flooded with artificial oestrogens, from the pill, together with the second chakra problems, led to a break down in the skin cells (cellulitis) which was further aggravated by problems in the third and fourth chakras.

The third chakra was a mess. All of the abdominal organs were very badly affected on both primary (personal power issues) and secondary (emotional) levels. The liver (fear) was poorly functioning, the gall bladder (anger) was totally blocked causing major disruption to the digestion, the spleen (frustration) was poorly functioning both digestively and in terms of the lymph tissue to the lower body. It was the lymph tissue which was responsible for many of her symptoms especially some of the digestive ones. The pancreas (emotional force) was disrupted in several ways. She was not producing digestive enzymes, her blood sugar balance was out and the hormones to the brain were disrupted leading to the dizzy spells. The constant blocking up of the intestines (old emotional "debris") had caused a small hole to form in the small intestines which was leaking a small quantity of bacteria into the abdomen (peritonitis). The long term use of antibiotics had killed off most of the useful bacteria in the intestines further adding to her digestive problems.

The fourth chakra was also a problem on both its primary level (the link from the soul to the physical body) and on its secondary level (how we express love). The whole of the endocrine system (hormone) was out of balance. This is the mechanism used by the soul in its primary connection with this chakra. By shutting herself away from the situation with her mother and step father, this link had been disrupted. The thymus gland and upper body lymphs were also totally blocked. The cellulitis problem also stemmed from a bacterial infection becoming locked into the immune system which could not clear it as the thymus and spleen were not fully functional. The sores in the nose and the vaginal dryness were also part of the same problem.

The fifth chakra (self expression) was disrupted because she felt she could not talk about her experiences and problems very easily. This led, together with the dysfunctional immune system, to a constant sore throat and node growths.

Where to start with such a combination of problems? The first place is with a giveaway beginning as far back into her past as she could remember. All of her problems stemmed from being blocked from expressing herself on the second, third, fourth and fifth chakras. By removing the accumulated debris of her unexpressed self, through the giveaway, her body's own recovery mechanisms could begin to function and bring her systems back to their correct balance. She had begun to look at many of her issues and find ways of making practical changes within her life. She found her job, although very stressful, very rewarding which helped with her self esteem (fourth chakra) and was beginning to give her a sense of security (first chakra). Her immune system problems would also be helped by beginning a course of the herb echinacea. We also suggested switching to an organic diet to boost her vitamin and mineral intake.

Although these symptoms appear to be extremely severe, once you begin the healing process, bringing the body's energies back into balance, the body will repair itself. Even conditions such as the minor tear in the intestines will heal by themselves if given a chance.

Case Twenty Three
A man in his fifties.

Medical History:
Several months previously he had a sudden pain in the abdomen followed by a discharge of blood from the rectum. The initial medical diagnosis was for haemorrhoids. The same thing occurred several weeks later which resulted in a revised diagnosis of bowel cancer.

Family History:
He had married a number of years ago and had three children. However, he gradually realised that he was gay and, when his children had reached adulthood, he had obtained a divorce. He had been a successful businessman with a flourishing business which he lost as part of the divorce settlement. He was very happy with a new partner but his father had died recently and this had upset him greatly.

Our Findings:
Cancer is really only another disease in the soul's armoury. Cancer only occurs as a last warning that there is an aspect of our lives that needs to be attended to. In this case, the emotional turmoil of literally having to "bury" himself away, who he truly was as a person, for many years meant that he needed to break away from his old life and begin to express himself in a way more appropriate to himself. By living a life that was totally against who he truly was, he lost all of his personal power. The body had hidden many of his symptoms until his father died, taking the tightly held emotional "debris" to breaking point, leading to the cancer.

In making the changes to his life with his new partner, accepting himself as he was, and then coming to terms with his father's death, he had actually switched off the whole cancer mechanism and his body was recovering by itself (for our findings on the mechanism of the whole cancer process see "*Everything You Always Wanted To Know....etc*").

As a foot note to this case history. This was an extremely dapper man who took great care of his appearance. The idea of bowel surgery and having to live with a colostomy bag for the rest of his life filled him with horror. Some weeks after his visit to us, he returned to his doctors to have himself discharged as he felt so much better and all of his symptoms had gone. The doctors insisted that the surgery proceeded and frightened him so much with their dire predictions of his future fate without surgery that he was pressurised into the surgery after all. Despite his insistence that all was well, the surgery was carried out and he now has a colostomy bag.

The liver is all about fear. The fear generated by the doctors' predictions of the progression of his illness is the reason why illnesses, especially cancers, transfer into the liver. If conditions such as cancer were better understood by the medical profession, liver complications would not arise.

Case Twenty Four
A man in his fifties.

Medical History:
A history of very bad headaches centred over the nose and right eye, about a year previously they had become much worse with constant pain and great heat to the right side of the head together with a constant, searing pain to the neck and shoulders. The vision to the left eye was constantly blurred and the eye was quite painful especially upon waking in the morning. Blood tests showed there was virtually no hydrocortisone in the blood (a hormone produced in the body which helps to guard against inflammation and pain). A few months ago an MRI scan had shown a benign tumour on the pituitary gland. He was taking a number of artificial hormones daily (prescribed by his GP) which seemed to help these conditions although he would need to take these for the rest of his life.

Family History:
A successful businessman with his own business which he was in the process of expanding. He had several children who always looked to him to remove them from their own difficulties, especially financial. He was very interested in developing himself "spiritually" and had belonged for a number of years to a "sect" who believed in developing the sixth chakra (the third eye). He had also attended several workshops designed to help him clear out his emotional problems and to open the fourth (heart) chakra.

Our Findings:
To start with the simpler symptoms. The shoulder problems very strongly linked into the first chakra. Between his business and his children, he was feeling quite insecure and this manifested itself in the shoulder muscles as he was quite literally "shouldering" too much responsibility. With the shoulder muscles becoming very tight, they caused the neck pain and most of his headache problems.

As people who teach healing, we encourage the use of meditations to enhance psychic capabilities (sixth chakra) and spiritual practices. However, as we can "see" the energies of the chakras and the effects that these types of meditation have upon them, we have developed meditations that are designed to work with and enhance all of the chakras.

Many western meditation techniques have been borrowed from a variety of Eastern traditions where meditations designed to enhance one chakra have been in use for many centuries. Unfortunately, in the translation from East to West, there is sometimes a loss of the understanding of the original purpose and uses of such meditations.

With the meditation practised by this client, only the sixth chakra was worked on. The meditation involved adding a huge amount of energy into the chakra but then it was not made use of. Over the years that this client had been meditating in this way, he had not actually used the enhanced energy of this chakra for any particular purpose. This resulted in a huge energy imbalance and led directly to the organs connected to this chakra becoming grossly dysfunctional. This chakra links directly into the left eye and the pituitary gland. Over the years, his meditation practices had forced huge quantities of energy into these organs and the vision defect and the pituitary tumour had resulted (the pituitary gland controls the balance of many of the body's hormones).

In addition to this problem, he had taken a workshop with the specific intention of opening the heart chakra (fourth chakra). With the imbalance already existing in the sixth chakra, the sudden injection of a huge quantity of energy into the fourth chakra, in his words, "blew a fuse" and the whole of his endocrine (hormone) system collapsed as a result.

Meditations are generally extremely helpful but, as with everything else, working with energies in an unbalanced way, especially over a long period of time, can result in huge energy imbalances and even damage to physical systems.

Having cleared the problems and put his energy system back into balance, we suggested that he begin a new meditation which energised and balanced all of his chakras equally. We would suggest that everyone who meditates to use this meditation to energise and balance the chakras properly.

Start in a comfortable position and relax as you would for your normal meditation practice. Once relaxed, begin to form a small point of concentration a short distance above your head. Begin to expand this point and put all of your concentration into it. Next, move this point of concentration all the way down the spine to the first chakra.

Begin to fill the region with a clear and as bright a copper gold as you can imagine and, as you do so, the colour begins to spin. It forms into the shape of a vortex with the point connected to the spine (coccyx) and the cone opening directly downwards in a line with the spine (see the illustration in chapter two). As it spins, the colour becomes brighter and clearer, the clearer the colour the faster the spin. As it spins, "ribbons" of colour begin to appear from the point of the vortex. The ribbons are made up of three colours, clear gold, violet and petrol blue.

Next, move the point of concentration up to the second chakra. This time, the point of the vortex is still connected to the spine but the vortex forms two cones equally front and back. The colour is petrol blue and spinning very fast equally front and back of the spine. As it spins, ribbons of three colours begin to appear from the point of the vortex. The colours are clear gold, violet and the copper gold of the first chakra.

Next, move the point of concentration up to the third chakra. The vortex shapes are equal front and back of the spine. The colour this time is petrol green. As the vortex spins, ribbons of clear gold, violet and petrol blue appear from the point of the vortex.

Move the point of concentration up to the fourth chakra. The vortex is equal front and back of the spine and is totally transparent with random flecks of clear gold. As the vortices spin random flecks of all of the other colours appear (clear gold, violet, copper hold, petrol blue and petrol green).

Move the point of concentration up to the fifth chakra. The fifth is the same as the fourth but totally transparent, without the clear gold flecks in the background, and with a lesser number of flecks of the other colours than the fourth

Move up to the sixth chakra. The sixth is the same as the fifth but with a lesser number of coloured flecks.

When you arrive at the seventh chakra, it changes slightly. The seventh chakra points directly upwards with the point of the cone on the top of the head on a direct line with the spine. The colour is transparent, just pure energy. The chakra just needs to spin as fast as you can make it. Once spinning, bring it back down the spine connecting into all the the chakras in turn. Once you have reached the first chakra and added the clear shimmer into the copper gold, all of the chakras will be fully energised and fully balanced (see also chapter eight).

There is no need to "close down" after this meditation as your energy systems are as powerful and protective as you can possibly make them. Remember, ill health comes about because the chakras are depleted or closed. With this meditation, you are as energised and protected as you can be.

As a piece of homework for everyone, use your common sense and intuition as to which workshops you attend - not all deliver on their promise and always remember the word BALANCE.

Case Twenty Five
A man in his twenties.

Medical History:
A history of colitis (an inflammation of the large intestine - the colon) for about ten years leading to severe abdominal pain and chronic diarrhoea up to eight times per night with a large amount of blood in the stools. He has carried out an extensive study of the correct foods for his condition but they did not help very much.

Family History:
He was sent away to boarding school whilst very young where he was bullied. His parents came from families both sides of a religious ideological divide. They had eventually divorced but not before using him as the focus of their arguments. He was in business with his father in the family firm where he carried a huge amount of responsibility however, his father did not respect him within the business despite a number of major successes.

Our Findings:
The kidneys (first chakra - security), especially the right, were in poor shape. There was an infection in the kidney, ureter and the bladder which had been there for some time.

All of the abdominal organs were severely disrupted (third chakra, personal power) to the point where the lining of the intestines were beginning to break down. There were also three separate bacterial infections in the gut.

The thymus (fourth chakra, expressions of love towards self) was dysfunctional leading to an extremely weak immune system keeping the gut and urinary tract infections in place.

We suggested the giveaway, beginning as far back as he could remember to remove as much of the past emotional problems as possible. We also suggested a self assertiveness course to help him to regain some of his self esteem and regain some sense of security within himself.

Really, he needed to look at his position within his family firm. As his father was very much in control of the company, it was unlikely that this young man would have any real say until his father retired. Did he really want to be in this position for many years to come? If he stayed, his health problems would probably return very quickly and most likely become much worse. The soul will not allow us to put our lives into the total control of others and symptoms, such as those experienced by this man, will arise to alert us to the fact that we have gone too far in giving away our lives.

However, if he found new employment, preferably setting up his own company, many of his health problems would disappear of their own accord.

We also suggested some vodka. We know that this sounds strange but vodka is a pure spirit and we have found very little that can remove the residue of bacteria out of the intestines any better (there is also an extract of grapefruit seed, called Citricidal, which works almost as well as it is a natural antibiotic which, like vodka, does not kill off useful bacteria). The dosage of vodka we normally suggest is a double measure (one third of a gill or 47 cl) per night for two or three nights. If you cannot tolerate neat vodka, the same volume of tonic water can be added to each dose (any other mixer negates the effect of the vodka).

Chapter Six

Reading The Symptoms

In the last few chapters, we have looked at specific case histories to try to illustrate how illness can be tracked back to a connected chakra. The process can appear to be a little complicated but all that it really needs is a slight change of focus and seeing the body in a slightly different way to the one which most of us are used to.

A medical diagnosis can seem to be quite complicated. Medical descriptions of illnesses tend to be expressed in terms which are not very easy to understand. Then you have to try and link the illness to specific organs and then try to work out what the illness actually means. It need not be this complicated if you relate the symptoms to one or more chakras.

The case histories given up until now have provided the medical diagnosis and related that diagnosis to the organs involved in the illness itself but, we have also given the chakra which relates to the illness and that is all that is really needed.

Over the past few decades we have seen an increase in the complexity of medical descriptions. As modern medicine has begun to use more and more sophisticated machinery for diagnosis and, combining this with a greater understanding of the physical mechanisms of the building blocks of an illness or disease, we have been caught up in the apparent complexity of the illness and begun to see illness as something which is outside of our grasp of understanding or control. Illness is not really very complicated in its root cause, it is the choice of words used by the doctors to describe what they see that makes the complications occur.

Let us take a closer look at the medical description of how an illness occurs - for the purposes of this exercise we will use the disease diabetes mellitus (which most of us know just simply as diabetes).

The medical description is this:
A disease in which the supply of insulin is insufficient for the body's needs. Insulin is a peptide hormone produced in the beta cells of the Islets of Langerhans in the pancreas. Insulin facilitates and accelerates the movement of glucose and amino acids across cell membranes. The beta cells constantly monitor the blood glucose levels and produce insulin in response to any drop in the glucose levels. Insulin also controls the activity of certain enzymes within the cells concerned with carbohydrate, fat and protein metabolism. Metabolism is the process of absorption of nutrients through the walls of specific cells, in this case, the cells of the villi of the small intestine.

Type 1 diabetes mellitus results from the destruction of the insulin producing cells in the pancreas by an auto immune process possibly triggered by a virus infection [an auto immune process is where the body no longer recognises a part of itself and begins to destroy cell structures as though they were foreign bodies] - description in brackets added by us.

Type 2, or maturity onset, diabetes mellitus is due to a relative insufficiency of insulin along with impaired sensitivity to the actions of insulin. Obesity, which necessitates larger quantities of insulin, is also a factor.

Insulin stimulates the passage of glucose from the blood through cell membranes into the cells to be utilised as fuel. In the absence of insulin the muscles are deprived of fuel, and sugar accumulates in the blood and is excreted into the urine, taking much water with it. There is excessive urination, dehydration and great thirst. Protein and fats are consumed as fuel. The muscles waste and dangerous acidic compounds called ketone bodies are formed. These can cause diabetic coma and death. Ketones are a class of acidic organic compounds that include acetone and aceto-acetic acid. Ketones have a carbonyl group, CO, linked to two other carbon atoms. They are formed in states of carbohydrate deficiency such as starvation or in conditions, such as diabetes mellitus, in which carbohydrates cannot be normally utilised. Acetone, aceto-acetic acid and beta-hydroxybutric acid are called ketone bodies. Ketones are volatile substances and confer on the breath the sickly, fruity odour of nail varnish remover.

Diabetes mellitus has many serious complications, especially bleeding within the eyes from retinopathy, kidney degeneration and obstruction of large blood vessels.
(This description was taken from *Collins Dictionary of Medicine* by Robert M. Youngson)

However, this is not the whole story. Medical dictionaries tend to have only a limited description of the function of organs within their descriptions of how bodily processes actually work. To understand the full mechanism of this illness, we have to dig a little deeper into the medical description. The following is an extract from an anatomical book written by Wynn Kapit and Dr Lawrence Elson. This is a description of the endocrine function of the pancreas.

The islands (islets) of endocrine tissue (and their capillaries) in the pancreas are surrounded by masses of grape like clusters/follicles of exocrine gland cells. The secretions of these cells enter ducts that are tributaries of the pancreatic ducts opening into the duodenum.

The islets are characterised by three or four different cell types. Alpha (A) cells, generally located in the periphery of the islet, secrete glucagon, a polypeptide hormone that binds to glucogen receptors on liver cell membranes. Glucagon induces the enzymatic breakdown of glycogen to glucose, a process called glycolysis. Glucagon also facilitates the formation of glucose from amino acids in the liver, a process called gluconeogenesis. As a result of this process, blood glucose levels increase.

Beta (B) cells, constituting 70% of the islet cell population, occupy the central part of the islet and secrete insulin, a polypeptide, primarily in response to increased plasma levels of glucose. Most insulin is taken up by the liver and kidney, but almost all cells can metabolise insulin. Insulin expedites the removal of glucose from the circulation by increasing the number of proteins that transport glucose across cell membranes in muscle cells, fat cells, leukocytes, and certain other cells (not including liver cells). Insulin increases the synthesis of glycogen from glucose in liver cells. Uptake of insulin is facilitated by insulin receptors (proteins) on the external and internal surfaces of many - but not all - cell membranes. Decreased insulin secretion or decreased numbers of activity of insulin receptors leads to glucose intolerance and/or diabetes mellitus.

The effects of insulin activity are far reaching: mediating electrolyte transport and the storage of nutrients (carbohydrate, proteins, fats), facilitating cellular growth, and enhancing liver, muscle and adipose tissue metabolism. [adipose tissue is a collection of fat cells which store excess nutrients for future use and to give the body insulation against the cold]

The full chakra diagnosis for diabetes mellitus would be:

Essentially, what the medical descriptions given above amount to is that there has been a breakdown in communication between the liver and the pancreas and the body's supply of fuel (glucose) has been disrupted.

Both the liver and the pancreas are controlled by the third chakra. The third chakra's primary function is with personal power whilst its secondary function is the emotions. The liver is the central processor for the emotions. All of our emotions pass through the liver and are then distributed to their appropriate organs. The liver also deals with the most powerful of our emotions, fear, jealousy and guilt. The pancreas is closely linked into the liver and deals, on an emotional level, with the amount of force we use to express our personal power issues and emotions - how forceful we are at expressing ourselves on this level.

Someone who has diabetes mellitus is someone who is afraid to express themselves as fully as they know they should. This fear is usually so great that they start to gnaw away at themselves from the inside out, literally denying their body food. From their viewpoint, it becomes a question of "I am afraid of expressing my wants and needs fully and I must make myself as small as possible so that others do not ask me my opinion".

The best way of breaking this pattern of thought, and healing the condition, is to take self assertiveness or self awareness classes to build up your own self esteem and image. These classes will help you to be more assertive in situations where you would have normally given away your personal power. As always, the giveaway process will help to clear some of the past emotional problems that brought about the problem in the first place, but the best option is to face the situation. The giveaway is brilliant, but there is no substitute for regaining your personal power - do not be fearful about fully expressing your emotional wants.

So, this is how simple and straight forward finding the root causes behind health problems can be. If you have a medical diagnosis, ask your doctor or consult a medical dictionary to determine the organs involved in your condition, then relate these organs to their corresponding chakra and use the descriptions and links given in chapter two to work out which region or regions of your life need to have some attention paid to them.

If you do not have a medical diagnosis but know that you have some kind of health problem, start by looking at where you feel the symptoms, then relate that part of your body to its corresponding chakra and this will give you the general region of your life which brought about the originating problem and where to start your self healing process.

As a side note, and as a way to illustrate how attending classes can help in unexpected ways, as far as our self esteem and personal power issues are concerned, here's a story about a friend of ours.

She decided to attend a five rhythms dance class held at a local college - innocent enough it would appear. The teacher had a few ideas of her own for incorporation into the dance movements. These involved different forms of expressing who you were as an individual within the steps of the five aspects of the dance. After the first class, our friend was extremely reluctant to return to the classes as she found the forms of expression started to strip away many of her defensive walls, however, following a certain degree of fortification with fermented grapes, she returned (brave woman).

About half way through the course, the teacher suggested that the pupils wrote a poem. This all seemed innocent enough until they turned up for the next class, poem in hand, and the teacher asked that each person, in turn, stood up in front of the class (about forty pupils) and "dance their poem". Our friend managed it. She doesn't know how she found the courage and neither does anyone else, but she did. Since then, she has not been afraid to confront anything or anybody.

From then on, we have always felt that if you can "dance your poem", you can do anything!

Chapter Seven
Past Life Cases

Approximately five percent of all of the clients we see have a problem which has a past life connection. This sounds like quite a number of people but it isn't really. Many people would like to pass their current health problems off as having a past life connection ("it's my karma") but that is to deny responsibility for their current lives and their current situations.

However, there are those who have brought a problem with them and this has given rise to the medical profession calling these types of illness genetic defects. In one sense, there is no such thing as a genetic defect whilst in another, everything that occurs within the body is genetically based. We also have a major conflict within the scientific world where on one side there are many millions of pounds and many millions of man hours being spent and planned to be spent on mapping the entire human geno because we are all the same and yet, on the other side, we have genetic evidence used in courts of law because every person's genetic make up is unique to themselves. From a scientific viewpoint, which one is the con?

The truth, as far as we are concerned, is that our individual genetic structures break down into three very distinct sections. Approximately fifteen percent of the DNA sequences determine the cell structures of the physical body (which cells become liver cells or eye cells, for example), a further ten percent we inherit from our parents (colour of hair, colour of eyes, shape of nose, for example), the remaining seventy five percent of all of our genetic material is our own. These gene sequences are our memories, every single thing that we have ever done or ever been is stored away in our primary memory structures, our unique DNA (see also chapter twelve).

The way in which these kinds of memories become transferred from one life to the next is determined by how powerful an experience was. If there was a severe trauma at the end of a previous lifetime, the "shock" to the physical elements of the soul can be so great that instead of the memory being locked away within our DNA spirals, it can be powerful enough to imprint itself into our current physical make up. A prime example of this is with the huge increase in children suffering from asthma. From our researches it would appear to have very little to do with car pollution, although that does not help, but these are souls being reborn after the trauma of being gassed in the trenches of the First World War.

As a general rule, strong illnesses which arise in childhood can often be from a past life cause, especially where such illnesses moderate or disappear at puberty. Illnesses which arise after puberty are always due to causes in this current life, except for bodily functions which are not viable before puberty such as pregnancy.

We have included six case histories here to try to illustrate the range of problems which can be generated by past life situations, the first case history is a perfect illustration of how the process works.

Case Twenty Six
A woman in her forties.

Medical History:
She contracted a yeast, candida type, infection in her bowel at

age eighteen which was not diagnosed or treated for almost twenty years leading to a number of complications. She had a history of ME type symptoms going back about eleven years which kept her energy levels very low. There was also a history of mild infections which were very slow to clear and a sensitivity to most chemical substances including normal domestic cleansers, with a more severe reaction to mercury in amalgam fillings and the organo phosphates found in flea sprays for pets. Her system had become so sensitive to chemicals that even petrol fumes caused major problems.

Family History:
At quite a young age her father, who she loved deeply, had died. This death resulted in her moving from her family home, which she loved, and her school and her school friends who she was also deeply fond of. She lived with her mother who she did not get on with on any level and she was deeply unhappy about the new area her mother had brought her to live. As soon as she was able, she moved as far away from her mother as she could.

Our Findings:
Her immune system was, effectively, not functioning neither was her endocrine system. The endocrine system is one of the body's most important systems as it is the body's hormonal balance. The organs linked to this system are: the pineal gland, the thyroid and parathyroid glands, parts of the pancreas, the adrenal glands and the sex hormone producing glands. The whole system is kept in balance by the hypothalamus and the pituitary gland. On a chakra level, the endocrine system is controlled by the fourth (heart) chakra's primary function, the link between the higher elements of the consciousness and the physical body.

The events surrounding her father's death in her childhood had literally broken her heart. The three elements surrounding the one incident occurring in less than one year had so shocked her system that it had totally disrupted the energies of the fourth chakra, severing the chakra's primary link. This had made the endocrine system go into a slow but steady decline disrupting every single element and system of the body. She could not fight infection nor could she fight off harmful substances so her body stored all of these toxins within the body's tissue, gradually breaking them down.

This is the process by which people die of a broken heart.The shock of the event had been so great that it had left a "scar" on the soul so deep that it imprinted itself into her primary genetic structures. In this life it meant that whatever treatment she received for her health symptoms, they would ultimately fail because as far as her body was concerned, the scarring was a fundamental part of her body's make up and would throw off any attempts to heal illness. In any future life, the scarring would imprint itself upon her new body's primary genetic structures, creating the same symptoms (we have treated several clients for precisely this problem).

This is the type of event sequence that can cause such a deep scarring to the consciousness that they become imprinted into the DNA sequencing creating a similar pattern of energetic weaknesses in a subsequent physical body. In other words, how events from a past life can transfer themselves into a future life.

Her father dying and the other changes that took place around the same time meant that she found difficulty in expressing love to anyone or anything. By forgiving her mother for the way in which she had been treated, her mother after all, made choices which she had felt appropriate at the time against the background of the death of the mother's husband and her sense of security also being lost, meant that the hurt to this woman was not an intentionally harmful act by the mother. If this woman can learn how to forgive the world and give her love to it, and those around her, unconditionally, the scar will heal and her body make a full recovery and the memories will remain within this current lifetime. A hard lesson and a difficult process, but it is only through this form of "letting go" of the events of the past that the scars can become fully healed and not be carried into a future life.

Case Twenty Seven
A woman in her thirties.

Medical History:
Severe and constant constipation since she was ten years old. There appeared to be no medical reason for the constipation and she has had to take laxatives ever since. She also had constant headaches and suffered from frequent bouts of depression and has had anorexia nervosa.

Family History:
Her parents are kind, open and loving and have tried to help her to deal with and understand her problems. She had lived and worked in several countries but always felt drawn to the USA. She felt out of her time and dressed as though from the 1940's.

Our Findings:
Physically the problem lay with a blocked spleen, gall bladder and her pancreas did not produce digestive enzymes (all organs connected with the third chakra - personal power). The whole of her endocrine system was out of balance (the primary function of the fourth chakra). Most importantly, there was an extremely strong memory within her system which locked her into the second world war. Our reading of this memory, including flashes of incidents she had seen for herself and recognised them for what they were, was this.

She had been born in 1916 in Britain. When the second world war began she had enlisted as a nurse and had somehow become seconded to the US army and stationed in the far east. In 1942 she had been caught up in an air raid and in trying to find a shelter, the jeep she had been driving had been blown up. On a soul level, she did not understand that she had died and that, as far as her genetic memory was concerned, she was still locked into 1942. The whole of her memory, soul and physical body was trying to function in an extreme conflict. She was alive but remembered dying. She remembered being born in 1916 and couldn't understand why she was so young and she could not remember the war ending or how she came back to Britain. An eighty year old time warp in a thirty year old body.

Part of her depression stemmed from her memories of the man she had loved in her previous life and she had great difficulty in reconciling herself to the fact that he had also died. A great part of her wished to die so that she could join him.

Another part of her problems came from the fact that she found current generations too noisy, bad mannered and crass. The generation she remembered were elegant, genteel and well mannered and she longed to return to the times she remembered as her youth.

Now that she had a greater understanding of her problems, our suggestion was that she wrote her autobiography. It was only through this kind of process that she could hope to piece the memories together and come to terms with who and where she was.

Case Twenty Eight
A woman in her thirties.

Medical history:
She had been having panic attacks for no apparent reason and they were causing considerable stress within her life.

Family History:
She came from a loving, professional family with a happy and fairly uneventful childhood. She had recently married and was looking to start a family.

Our Findings:
Upon questioning her, it became apparent that the panic attacks had begun when she had discussed starting a family with her new husband.

These attacks were linked to a previous lifetime in India in the 1500's. She had been a woman of high birth and had given birth to a disabled son in 1542. In Indian society, disabled children were frowned upon and cast out of the family either to die or to find their own life on the streets. In that lifetime, she had decided that she did not want to lose her son, despite his disabilities and the implications for her within her society. So, as she refused to dispose of her son, her family made her an outcast and disowned her. She spent the rest of that lifetime as a beggar shunned by her family and by the world around her.

In this lifetime, when the subject of her mothering children was raised, the memory of that previous life came to the fore and panic attacks resulted as, as far as her soul memory was concerned, she would automatically become a complete social outcast.

By helping her to understand that these panic attacks belonged to another life and another time, they began to subside and she decided to proceed with starting a family.

Case Twenty Nine
A woman in her forties.

Medical History:
ME type problems had begun about fifteen years ago with a virus that did not clear. The condition had become severe about three years ago and she had been virtually housebound since. She had wanted to have children but found that she could not become pregnant despite having an IVF treatment. There was constant muscle pain in her legs and arms. The situation had been aggravated some years ago when she had a whiplash type injury which had displaced the sacroiliac joint and created a painful neck problem.

Family History:
She was happily married to a man who was sympathetic to her problems and tried to help her as much as he could.

Our Findings:
The ME had begun about the time she and her husband began to think about a family. Her reproductive system appeared to be functioning normally but there were deficiencies in her progesterone/oestrogen balance. In this particular case there were two past life links, both associated with pregnancy.

In the first, she had been raped. This was in sixteenth century France where she had been a part of the French court and, although she moved in the highest social circles, the rapist had been a workman. The scandal that would have resulted would not have been tolerated by either her family or the court and the pregnancy had been forcibly terminated, leading to her death. This forcible termination and death generated the first wound in her genetic memory which was carried forward and affected her next life.

In the second, she was a settler in New England in the late seventeen hundreds. The pregnancy had gone reasonably well and she was very happy in her life despite being very isolated from other farmsteads. Ultimately, the pregnancy turned into a breach birth and as there was no medical help available, she had died along with her child.

In this lifetime, when the subject of children was raised, her genetic memories took over and prevented pregnancy by altering her hormonal balance.

As with most past life problems, by helping our clients to understand that their problems are not brought about by a physical problem (related to present life chakra imbalances), but memories of a time which no longer exists, the memory can be released and the physical symptoms removed.

Her soul wanted her to remove the past life memory and have her family. As she had decided not to investigate and clear these memories, her soul had put her life on hold until she did, bringing about her ME symptoms. ME is caused by the pineal gland producing too much of the hormone melatonin. This hormone is the trigger that tells us to go to sleep at night or to wake up in the morning. If we go against the wishes of the soul, it will stimulate the pineal and ME symptoms produced until a resolution for the problem is found.

The whiplash injury came about in the region of the second chakra, reflecting the weakened state of this region of her life with the conflict surrounding the subject of childbirth.

Case Thirty
A woman in her late thirties.

Medical History:
A history of IBS (Irritable Bowel Syndrome) type symptoms

together with a feeling of emotional strain and blockages. Despite a number of attempts at resolving her health problems in a number of ways, she always ended up feeling that she was fighting herself. There was also a history of gaining weight which no diet would remove.

Family History:
She tended to act as the peacemaker within a very fractious family and had done so all her life. She had been attempting to expand on a "spiritual" front but always felt blocked from moving in this direction.

Our Findings:
On a physical level, the following organs were not functioning as well as they could be: the gall bladder (third chakra, personal power - relating to suppressed anger); the thymus (fourth chakra - expressions of love towards self); the thyroid was under active (fifth chakra - being blocked from saying what you think); the pituitary gland (sixth chakra - a from of withdrawal from the physical world). But, underlying all of these physical symptoms was a very powerful memory.

This was all about a past life in France in the mid 1700's. This had been a life of quite severe deprivation. She had survived through several cycles of starvation and plenty and it had left her with a very keen sense of "saving for a rainy day". Whenever there was a sense of plenty, she would hoard it against a time when the things she required were not so plentiful. In this lifetime, the memory had translated into a sense that "the sky was about to fall" and so she must always eat against starvation and hold very tightly to her emotions and to those around her who she felt close to. By locking this pattern of behaviour into this life, she always wanted to resolve any family conflict as quickly as possible in case the issues were not resolved before the next disaster took her loved ones away. Her body responded to this memory by holding onto everything she ate, putting on as much weight as possible to prevent starvation in a future famine. On the emotional side, because she felt she had to resolve any conflicts with loved ones, she felt she could not express herself as forcefully as she knew she should for fear of causing further conflict.

All of these emotional conflicts disrupted most of the systems of the body and depleted the energies of several of the chakras. By helping her to see where her patterns of behaviour came from, it was possible to break these patterns and remove the problem memories.

Case Thirty One
A ten year old girl.

Medical History:
She sometimes experienced sleeping problems as her throat would constrict and she would have difficulty in breathing. The same form of throat constriction would occur whenever she was chased. This could be in sports activities at school or when chased in play. In these instances, she would feel a lump build in her throat and she would black out from lack of oxygen. There was no clear medical diagnosis and the next stage was investigative open heart surgery.

Family History:
A close, warm, loving family who were baffled and concerned about her condition. The girl was very psychic and clairvoyant which her family did not try to stop. She had also had memories of past lives which she found natural and fascinating but none of them had any bearing on her symptoms. As an aside, her mother had two miscarriages before giving birth to this girl. The girl frequently spoke of seeing and communicating with two "sisters" with whom she played.From our viewpoint, she was a lovely, warm and open little girl who instantly took our hearts.

Our Findings:
There was a slight weakness to the arterial walls of the artery from the heart to the brain and an inflammation of the diaphragm but, other than these very mild symptoms, nothing.

However, there was a very powerful memory. She had been a wise woman, the village herbalist and midwife in Britain in the mid 1600's. When the medical profession began to clear out any opposition to their dominance in the healing business, she had been branded a witch. One day, the witch hunters came to try her and she was chased and hung.

The memory of these events had been so strong that every time she was chased her body would remember the final outcome and her throat would constrict leading to her blacking out. Sometimes the memory would surface as she was relaxing as she went to sleep and her body would respond.

Working with children with these kinds of problems is very interesting. If adults have these kinds of memories then they will have lived a number of years with these memories colouring their present life, allowing the patterns of behaviour imposed by these memories to become a part of this lifetime.

With children, however, they have not lived long enough for these patterns to have become established and removing these memories can have very dramatic effects. In this case, we did not tell the girl all of our findings (we did fully discuss the problem with her parents), we just deactivated the memory within her genetic structures and the symptoms disappeared overnight and have not returned.

We do not remove these kinds of memories as they belong to the individual we are working with and are an intrinsic part of that individual's make up. What it is possible to do is to take the memory off the "active" list and allow the body to settle into a more natural rhythm.

A note to all parents. If your child claims to have memories of past lives, or claims to play with the faerie, please listen to them and try to encourage such children in their beliefs. A great deal of psychological damage can be done to children by stifling their understanding of the not quite so physical world.

Case Thirty Two
A ten year old girl.

Medical History:
There were problems with both of her ears. Her rib cage hurt when she lay down and there would be quite a lot of pain around her ribs if she sat upright for any length of time. X-rays taken of the shoulder and ribs looked as though she had broken the shoulder at some time but no one in her family knew when such an injury could have occurred. The shoulder was slightly malformed and the muscles, nerves and bones were not properly formed.

Family History:
Everyone was baffled by her problem and her apparent injury.

Our Findings:
The ear problems came from nerve pressures caused by the shoulder and rib injuries.The rib injuries did not take place in this lifetime. The memory was of a time in South Africa where she had been crushed in a rock fall. A very large boulder had landed on her right side totally crushing the shoulder and upper rib cage, killing her. The memory of the trauma had been very strong and when her consciousness had built her body for this lifetime, the imprint of the injury was built into her rib cage and shoulder.

From our viewpoint, this case was quite intriguing. There were no actual deformities or abnormalities in her rib cage or shoulder. The actual damage site was like looking at a photograph of the past life injury, basically a flat sheet with an image imposed upon it. The image was of a crushed shoulder, crushed ribs, damaged muscles and nerves, strong enough to show up on an x-ray and the nerve structures for her current body were interwoven into the image causing the rib and shoulder pain. By removing the "photograph", the body settled down, the nerves and muscles settled into the patterns of her current body and the pains have now gone.

*****

In the last couple of years, we have encountered a new form of twist on past life connections between people. The next chapter details a change of energy which is having many far reaching implications for everybody on the planet. It is because of these energy changes that this particular problem has been brought to light.

Most people are familiar with the expression "soul mate". This expression is usually taken to mean that a new someone who has come into your life, or the one you are searching for, is the person of your dreams, the one who fits within your world so closely that everything must be right. This is not necessarily the truth of the situation.

There are occasions where we find ourselves so closely connected with someone that we promise to "always look after them" on some level. These expressions of life long support can sometimes create situations which extend beyond that particular life. If the promise of constant, everlasting support is made with sufficient impetus and the person receiving that promise wholeheartedly accepts it, a link can be formed between the two souls concerned at a level which goes far beyond the physical.

In the past, these links have not necessarily been that much of a problem. However, with our consciousness integration process well under way, these high level links are beginning to become something of a problem. They can also, in very rare instances, bring about health problems that are nothing to do with the one experiencing them.

There have always been thirteen chakras. Seven within the physical body and six that extend to form the link with the higher levels of our consciousness. Where these links have been formed they are formed in the higher six chakras. Depending upon the strength of the promise, the link can be anywhere from the eighth chakra to the thirteenth. As we undergo our integration process, drawing the energies of the six higher chakras into the physical, these links can act like "knots" in the energy flow and the integration process stopped.

For example, we came across one situation where a link was formed between two brothers during a period of early Greek history. Both were athletes in the first Olympic games and a bond was formed between them which led to one of these high level links being formed on the ninth chakra. The brother who came to see us was aware of his own energy changes and the further potential for change but knew that somewhere he was blocked from further progress. In energy terms, he was about 40% through the first phase of change. When we removed the link with his brother he instantly accelerated to 100%. The link was acting literally like a knot and was preventing any further energy integration.

In another case, a husband and wife knew that there was something between them which was slowing down their lives, a sense of not being able to progress even though they were very happily married and ran a successful business together. Part of their problem was that the husband felt unable to make any kind of major decision by himself, he always had to defer to his wife. Whilst this was not a major problem, both were beginning to feel that there was something underlying this lack of taking responsibility as they had tried to overcome it.

Their problem stemmed from a lifetime they had shared in early Egypt. He was living as a woman at the time and had been promoted to the role of high priestess. At the time, he felt he could not take on that level of responsibility and had asked a close companion (his present wife) to share the responsibility of the job. In taking on this share of the role, his partner had made a promise along the lines of "I will always help you with situations of responsibility where you feel unable to cope". This promise had formed a link at the twelfth chakra and had remained there ever since. In this lifetime, these two "soul mates" had come together to try to resolve the responsibility issue but found that the link was too strong for them to break by themselves. We managed to break the link and both felt a great sense of release. Breaking the link did not affect their marriage except, if anything, it brought them closer together as there was no longer any issue to be resolved between them.

Unfortunately, slowing down the energy flow is not the only problem these high level links can cause.

We have encountered a few links where the promise has been made on a more emotional level. The kind of promise made was along the lines of "you have been hurt by the situation and so I will always help you with any emotional hurts".

Where such links as these are formed, they can have a direct effect upon the one making the promise in terms of their health. We have encountered several such cases where health problems have arisen for no apparent cause.

The best example we found of this type of link was where a woman had several second and third chakra problems which could not be tracked to her behaviour. The problems had not been particularly serious in the past but were now rapidly deteriorating.

She had recently taken a new job where she met a man with whom she felt an instant rapport. There were no sexual connections with this "soul mate", just a relaxed, comfortable recognition. It was when their friendship began that her health problems became worse.

When we began to work on her system, the link came to light. The link had been made very many lifetimes ago when both of them were facing major changes to their lives. Our client had offered to help her friend through these changes and this emotional link was formed. In this lifetime, she was happily married and was very good at expressing her emotional needs but still ended up with health problems in the second and third chakra organs.

What was occurring was that the link was so strong that when her friend had difficulties in his life, the emotional problems were transferred through the link to our client. When they met, he was going through a very emotional time which should have caused him problems on the second and third chakra levels but all of this was dumped onto her through the link. Her health problems were now so bad that she was developing uterine cancer.

By bringing the two of them together, their respective souls were trying to find a way to resolve the whole situation and break the link. However, her health problems were becoming too immediate and so she consulted us. Once we broke the link, her energy levels shot up and the immediacy of her health problems lessened. They are both still friends but he is now learning to take responsibility for his own emotional problems.

*****

If you feel that you have a problem linked into a past life situation, probably the best way of investigating and removing these memories would be to visit a past life hypnotist/therapist. These are people who have experience of leading people back through their past lives to help them to understand and release the problem memories.

If you feel as though there is a "link" with another person, these need to be investigated very specifically with the regressionist in order for them to be broken.

Chapter Eight

Current Changes of Energy

Whilst the current energy changes are detailed in two of our previous books, "The Journey Home" and "The Fool's First Steps", these changes are having an effect upon the chakras and some interesting physical symptoms are occurring as a result and so we thought it appropriate to include a brief description here.

What do we mean by energy changes?
The whole purpose of human history, or at least the last seven thousand years of human karmic history, has been to find a way of integrating the whole of human consciousness into a physical human body. There are many reasons as to why we do not bring all of our consciousness into the physical and those are outside the scope of this book (see the books mentioned above), but what humanity as a whole is beginning to embark upon is the consciousness integration process.

This integration process has many repercussions and ramifications as far as we are concerned, leading to changes on so vast a scale that we have not experienced such a change in the whole of human history.

At our most fundamental level, we are energy. The consciousness is an energy, the physical tissues of the body are an energy and everything that surrounds us is an energy.

113

These energies are of particular frequencies but, as we begin our change, the energies that make us are changing. As described in chapter two, the chakras have a frequency which correspond to particular colours. These colours have traditionally been red, orange, yellow, green, blue, indigo and violet but, as we undergo our change, these colours also change. We are now well down the route that this change is taking us and the chakras now have new colours.

What you must remember is that the chakras are shaped like a vortex. From the side they look like an ice cream cone, with the point of the cone fixed to the spine. The first chakra's point is fixed to the base of the coccyx and the cone opens directly downwards. The second, third, fourth, fifth and sixth chakras have a vortex cone fixed on both sides of the spine with the vortex opening away from the body. The seventh chakra's point is fixed to the top of the head on a direct line with the spine with the cone opening directly upwards and away from the body. If you look at the chakra from the front, it is round and spinning very fast. The old colours look like a single, solid colour but spinning. The new colours have a base colour but mixed in with this are "flecks" of colour that come from the point and revolve around the vortex shape. Spirals of colours emanating from the central point.

The first chakra is now a bright copper gold with flecks of clear gold, petrol blue and violet.

The second chakra is a vivid "petrol" blue with flecks of clear gold, violet and copper gold.

The third is now vivid "petrol" green with flecks of clear gold, violet and petrol blue.

The fourth is transparent (no colour) with flecks of all the new chakra colours.

The fifth is the same as the fourth but with a lesser number of coloured flecks.

The sixth is the same as the fifth but with an even lesser number of coloured flecks.

The seventh is now totally transparent with no other colours. Pure energy.

Also see case twenty four in Chapter five for a meditation using these colours.

The changes of colour represent a change of energy frequencies by a factor of ten thousand. For example, the first chakra has traditionally had a frequency range of 7.56 cycles per second to 7.500 cycles per second. The first chakra needed to begin at 7.56 Hz as that coincided with the planet's own base frequency. If we did not match the frequency of the first chakra to the planet's, we would not be able to build the physical body. However, the planet itself is also undergoing a major change of energies and its base frequency was reset on the 14th June 2000 and is now 3.500 cycles per second. Consequently the human first chakra is now from 3 500 cycles per second to 75.000 cycles per second, a frequency higher than the old seventh chakra used to be. The energy of the seventh chakra goes up to at least 225.000 cycles per second. Words cannot describe what these colours look like, they are breathtaking.

Incidentally, the planetary energy change in June means that all animals and plants have also changed their base frequency otherwise they could not remain on the planet.

The human change was completed on the first of June 2000. What we mean by this is that the human etheric template, the energetic template used by the consciousness to build the human physical body, is now of the new chakra colours. This means that any new soul wishing to be human has to be able to incorporate the new chakra colours. It also means that anyone wishing to stay on the planet to complete their own consciousness integration must raise their energy frequencies from the old colours to the new. Anyone who is of the old frequencies, and does not change to the new, will not be able to stay on the planet. Everyone who has decided to stay physical must have incorporated all of the new colours by the middle of 2001 at the latest.

But, where is all of this extra energy coming from?
Traditionally, we have always thought that there were seven primary chakras. Whilst this is true for the physical body, this is not the whole picture. The rest of our consciousness, the higher self, comprises the remainder of our energies, which includes a further six chakras. This means that our total energy construction is comprised of thirteen chakras, or energy centres.

As we integrate the remainder of our consciousness into the physical body, these six "higher" chakras overlie the six lower chakras and the higher energy frequencies of the higher chakras are integrated into the six lower chakras, producing the change in colours. As these higher energies are integrated into the body, the higher self is then literally sitting on the top of the head ready to begin the second phase of change.

However, this is not the only change that is occurring. Along with this personal change are a range of other changes which are having a major impact upon our physical, energetic and genetic structures.

The change began at 6.00 pm BST on the 14th August 1996 with the final connection of the global primary energy centre. This energy connection activated the twelve other major global energy centres and energised the new planetary lay line grid.

These energy centres are often thought of as the Earth's chakras and, whilst this analogy is appealing, is not strictly true. The Earth does have its chakras but they belong to its own consciousness. These new energy centres are more to do with the energies supporting a change within humanity. These new energies have had a profound affect upon the planet but have brought about an even greater level of change within humanity as a whole.

The final connection of the primary energy centre (see *The Journey Home*) began a process of change to people which most are only now beginning to realise is occurring. It is this connection which began the change to our chakras. Along with the energy came a low level pulse which also began to alter the energy structures of our DNA, clearing the way for the next phase of human change.

At the end of 1996, between Christmas and the New Year, the learning process we have come to know as karma, stopped. This means that we are no longer building any complications into our future lives. What we have been doing since the beginning of 1997 is to clear out all of our unwanted accumulated debris.

In a period of four months, the whole world and human future history changed, and changed for the better. New energies, the cessation of karma and the beginning of the clearing of all of the past memories and complications.

As this change began, we saw the emergence of new illnesses which were unknown to the medical profession. If you think about what DNA is for a moment. DNA is our primary memory structure. Everything that we have ever been or ever experienced whilst we have been physical, is contained within our genes. This is what makes each of us genetically unique, we have unique memories which belong only to us. With the ending of karma, the knowledge gathering process, we could begin to clear the memories we no longer required, clearing the way for the remainder of our memories stored within the energies of the higher self.

As these memories, pieces of DNA, are released, they are cleared out of the body. However, if we have not fully dealt with all of the implications of that memory, as in cases 26 - 32 for example, these DNA memory sequences can become lodged in associated organs of the body and act like viruses. This is why the medical profession is increasingly floundering. Many of these new illnesses are not new illnesses, nor are they new viruses, they are old memories that we have not let go.

The stopping of karma has, literally, released us from the past. We are no longer building experience but clearing the past. All of the events that have occurred in the world, or on a personal level, since the beginning of 1997 have been to clear our past from our memories. As we clear these memories, we take on the new energies. The more energy we take on, the more we can clear. The more we clear, the more energy we take on. The more energy we take on, the more of our total self we can absorb. The more of our total self we can absorb, the more we build our new/old DNA of the total consciousness. In the not too distant future we will have recombined our original thirteen spirals of the DNA and brought the whole of the self into the physical. For the first time in modern human history we will be a complete consciousness in a physical body. It sounds remarkable, it sounds impossible but, we have all, collectively, taken the decisions that have led us to this point. We might not be consciously aware of the decision making process but we have all taken part in these decisions. This is why we all feel the need for change and why we are all feeling that we must take action to sort out our problems. In the past we could ignore our problems, even pass them forward to some future life where we might be more able to deal with those kinds of problem situations. This is no longer true. We have been seeing clients in our healing practice for some time now who know that they have to resolve their issues. It is no longer a question of it would be a good idea to clear their problems but a sense of urgency and of an imperative. The cause of this need for change is the change of energy, this change of us, clearing our past into a new future.

Having said all of this, there is no need to panic. All of us have made these decisions, individually and collectively and, on a higher level, we are all working towards our final clearances. All of us are doing this in our own way. Nobody can tell you what is the right or the wrong way, there is only your way. We have met people who have totally completed this first phase of change and are starting into phase two whilst we have met others who are only forty percent into the first phase of change. There are no hard and fast rules to this change, we are all working at our own pace and in our own ways. Whilst we must all complete our own personal changes by a particular date, we all have time to do what we need to do. Our higher selves are busily at work bringing these changes about and they can and will happen in a time scale appropriate to ourselves.

If you are feeling as though you have to make changes in your life, try not to fight them, try to accept them in as much as possible. We are in a world of enormous change and the change needs to occur. It is something we have all agreed to be a part of and something we are striving for. Trying to hold back will not work as the impetus is now too great.

If you find yourself with a strange illness which does not respond very well to treatment, do not panic. Look at where the illness is centred and understand it on a chakra level. The chakras are 100% accurate and foolproof if you are prepared to take an honest look at yourself. More often than not, all that is needed to resolve most of these cases is several serious uses of the giveaway. Ask yourself what the problem is and where does it lie within the body. Begin to write down what your feelings, thoughts and memories are, you will be surprised what comes out on the paper. Do not be afraid of the process, all you are investigating is the past, a past that you have already survived.

If you feel as though you are unable to unlock this past for yourself, there are many different types of practitioners available who can help - see the directory in the back of Everything You Always Wanted To Know About Your Body etc. and find one which appeals to you. We are all different with different needs, what works for one person will not necessarily work for another, but give it a try. The only danger in this process is that you will clear out your past and discover yourself.

The New Colours of Life
The first problem we encountered when trying to represent the new colours was which shape of outline to use. Eventually, we decided to use a crop formation. This particular one appeared in a field in Barbury Castle near Avebury in Wiltshire on the 15th April 1997. This formation appeared in a field of oil seed rape. Oil seed rape stalks are extremely delicate and cannot be bent into a shape as they snap, this means that this formation cannot be a fake. A very similar shape, but much more complex, appeared in a field in Hackpen Hill, near Broad Hinton in Wiltshire in early July 1999 which would also have been a suitable pattern to use but the formation was more complex and we could not work out the geometry sufficiently to use it as a base pattern.

The second problem we encountered was what type of paint or ink to use to give even an impression of the amazing qualities of these colours. Eventually we found a range of pearlescent acrylic inks which do the job quite well.

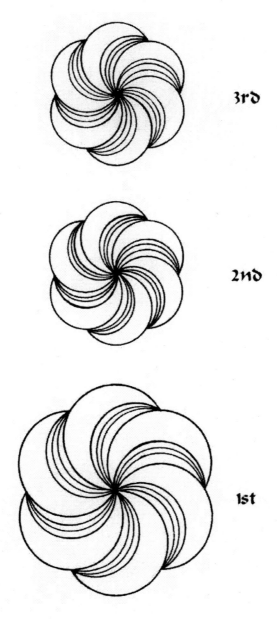

3rd

2nd

1st

The New Chakras From 1st to 3rd

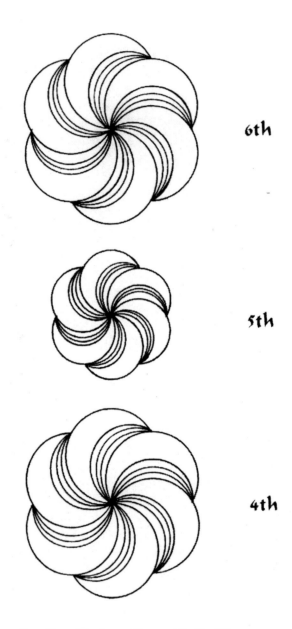

6th

5th

4th

The New Chakras From 4th To 6th

We have not printed the new chakras in colour as there are limitations to the printing process which would lose some of the qualities that need to be represented. So, if you photocopy or trace the images on the following two pages and proceed as follows.

The pearlescent inks we used are manufactured by Daler Rowney and are available from most good artists supply shops. The colours you will need are:
Birdwing Copper, Mazuma Gold, Silver Pearl, Moon Violet and Galactic Blue.

If you look at the illustrations, you will see that each chakra is divided into large segments and smaller segments which are divided into three. Each of the large segments will have a single colour and each of the "fins" of the smaller, divided segments will also have a colour.

The First Chakra
For the larger segments you need to mix together some of the Birdwing Copper and the Mazuma Gold in roughly equal quantities. Paint each of the larger segments in this coppery gold mixture.

Each of the fins of the smaller segments have their own colour. The first needs to be in Moon Violet, the second in Mazuma Gold and the third in Galactic Blue. Continue painting all of the fins of the smaller segments all of the way around the pattern in the same sequence of colours.

The Second Chakra
The larger segments of this chakra are all painted in Galactic Blue.

The fins of the smaller segments are painted Moon Violet for the first, Mazuma Gold for the second and the third is the copper gold mixture from the first chakra. Continue painting all of the fins in the same colour sequence all of the way around the pattern.

The Third Chakra

The larger segments are an equal mixture of Galactic Blue and Mazuma Gold mixed together to give a green. Paint all of the larger segments with this colour.

The fins of the smaller segments are painted in the following sequence. The first is in Moon Violet, the second in Mazuma Gold and the third in the blue from the second chakra. Continue painting all of the fins in the same colour sequence all of the way round the pattern.

The Fourth Chakra

The larger segments are actually transparent but we used Silver Pearl to give it the same "sheen" as the other colours. On to the transparent are random "flecks" of Mazuma Gold.

The fins of the smaller segments are all painted in the same way, flecks of the Moon Violet, Mazuma Gold, Galactic Blue, the green of the third chakra and the coppery gold of the first. In other words, all of the colours used so far.

The Fifth Chakra

The whole of the pattern is painted with the Silver Pearl. Onto this you will need to add random flecks of all of the colours used so far but a lesser number than the fourth chakra.

The Sixth Chakra

This chakra is coloured in exactly the same way as the fifth, a Silver Pearl background over the whole area, but with a lesser number of the coloured flecks.

We have not included an illustration of the seventh chakra as that is coloured with the Silver Pearl without any coloured flecks at all - transparent, totally pure energy.

There is also another level of change with these new chakra energies. Traditionally, all of the seven chakras have been of the same size reflecting that all had an equal part to play in our lives and our well being. With these new energies, the relationship of the chakras change. The first, fourth, sixth and seventh remain the same size but alter their energy frequencies, whilst the second, third and fifth reduce in size whilst they also change to the higher frequencies.

The size reduction is a reflection of the changing needs of our bodies and souls. The original seven chakras were needed to be of the same size as each held equal importance in our lives but the new colours reflect how our changing energies will alter our needs in our new world.

The second and third chakras have needed a great deal of energy to help us cope with the trials and tribulations of our sexual relationships and our emotional problems. As we change in our energies, we will become more honest in our dealings with others and problem areas of our lives, as represented by these two chakras, become much less and, therefore, they do not require so much energy.

The fifth chakra reduces in size to reflect our changing means of communication. The psychic communication centres within the brain are beginning to reactivate and so we will gradually change from physical speech to a more psychic form of communication.

However, along with these extremely positive changes also come ones which, in the short term, are providing some uncomfortable symptoms.

When we fall asleep and lie awkwardly on an arm, the blood stops circulating freely and we describe the arm as "fallen asleep". When we change position and the blood begins to flow normally again, we feel a sensation of "pins and needles" whilst the arm muscles and nerves are coming back to life.

This is the kind of situation we are currently facing. The psychic communication centres within the brain are located in four locations. If you take a line directly up from the back of the ear to just where the head changes from its side to its top, this is the start of one of the centres. The psychic centre begins at this point and extends towards the back of the head by about 2" (5cm) and is about " (2cm) deep. There is one of these centres located either side of the head. The other two centres are located at the base of the brain, one on either side of the bump just above the junction of the skull and the neck. As these psychic centres begin to re-energise, there is a flow of energy similar to the one described above for the blood flow returning to an arm that has been asleep. This new energy flow is forcing these psychic centres to expand and for the body to begin to pump blood into these regions. These new flows of blood and energy are putting pressure onto several regions of the skull.

The first region affected is the skull itself. As these psychic communication centres begin to return to life, they expand and the plates of the skull have to move very slightly to accommodate the expansion. If the skull plates have become fused, which they will be if you are over thirty, the plates are reluctant to move and this lack of movement can result in headaches which have no apparent cause. These headaches are usually centred at the skull plate joint just at the top of the bridge of the nose or, more usually, at the back of the skull where three plates meet. They can also be felt at the sides of the skull if the plates there do not have sufficient free movement in them - see the illustrations of the skull below.

The front and sides of the skull just tend to cause headaches localised to the region where the plates are "sticking" but the lack of movement at the back of the head can cause further problems.

Of The Skull
The muscles of the neck do not connect to the vertebrae of the neck but to a ligament (called the nuchal ligament) which spans from the top of the spine to the base of the skull. As the plates at the back of the head begin to expand, pressure is put onto this ligament and it tries to stretch. However, as it is a ligament with a number of muscles attached, it does not stretch easily and tensions in the neck muscles can result as well as severe headaches at the back of the head.

A further consequence of these regions of the brain returning to life is that the nerves that run to and from or alongside these regions can also be affected. One nerve, in particular, can have major short term consequences. This is the nerve that passes through the skull just in front of the psychic centres at the side of the head. It passes through the skull, connects into the nerve centre at the temples and extends down to the nerve centre where the upper and lower jaws meet. This nerve has to expand to accommodate these changes and it can also become trapped by the skull plates not moving freely. This nerve pressure can affect the back of the eyes and give headaches at the temples but it can also affect the jaw nerve centre and this is where most people are feeling it.

Where there is a problem with the jaws, it can manifest itself in several ways. The first is with toothache which seems to move around either jaw for no apparent reason. Dental x-rays do not show any problem but yet there is a great deal of pain. The second is the pain can be a general pain in the upper or lower jaw on either one side of the jaw or the other, or both. Both types of pain move around for no apparent reason.

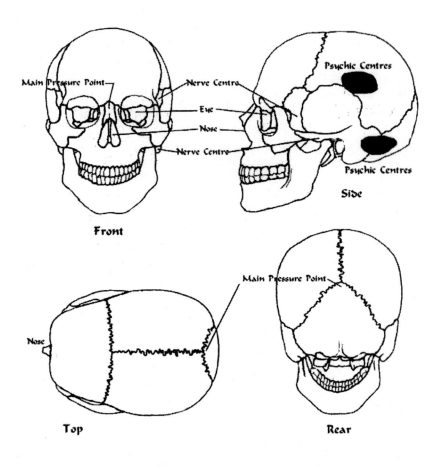

The Plates of the Skull

There are several ways of coping with these problems apart from taking painkillers.

Firstly, you can take a supplement of potassium. This is a mineral which the body uses to build nerves from. Taking the supplement will help the nerves to expand rapidly reducing the time taken for the body to adjust.

Secondly, you can seek out someone who can provide a head massage. This can help relieve the pressures between the plates and ease the pressure on the muscles and ligaments of the neck. Not everyone can cope with this kind of massage when they have a headache.

Thirdly, you can visit a cranial osteopath. These are specialists at manipulating the plates of the skull and helping to reduce pressure within or on the head. They do this very gently so it is rarely painful.

We are changing and we are changing at a pace which is rapidly accelerating. Nothing can now prevent this change from occurring and so all we can do is to go along with it. We have all chosen to be a part of this change and have all worked for many centuries to arrive at this point in time. You would not be alive on the planet at this time if you were not intending to be a part of this change.

This change is your legacy, your right, try to flow with it and everything will settle into place naturally. Try to fight the new energy and your body will let you know, very quickly, that it does not agree with you.

There is nothing to fear in these changes, we have just finished one job and are set to enjoy the fruits of all of our hard labours.

On a personal note.
As we have gone through these changes, we have noted several bodily responses which we thought you might be interested in.

First of all, the headaches, jaw aches and tooth aches do disappear. Much as it seems as though your head is going to explode or all of your teeth fall out, it doesn't and they don't! There can be a varying need for chocolate - so give it a try and stick to the organic.

The one bodily requirement which many will be resistant to is a need to consume heavy protein in the form of meat. If you are vegetarian, this can present a strong ethical dilemma.

The highest form of energy available from all foods is to be found in meat. This is not physical energy in the sense of being able to run etc. but energy in the way in which the body uses it to construct new cells. Most vegetarians are very adept at giving themselves a whole diet which the body can thrive on but, in the case of these changes, the body needs more help. Meat becomes essential and so we found that there are two types of meat sources available which overcome any objection to the treatment of the animals concerned.

The first is obviously organic meats. These animals are treated with the respect they deserve and are not treated with chemicals of any kind. The second is almost as good as organic. This is a form of meat produced from what is known as "traditionally reared" animals. A number of farms are now reverting to this form of rearing. This is where the animals are free ranging and are only treated with veterinary treatments if they become unwell. No chemicals are used other than these.

Our answer to these additional bodily requirements has been to go along with them, fighting or ignoring them brought their own complications. Ultimately, these changes are very positive so there is no need to fear. Just progress with them and if your body starts to demand something new or unusual, try to go along with it and your transition will become smoother. Ignore or deny these urges and the body responds quite strongly!

Chapter Nine

Case Histories

Strange But True!

In the last chapter we looked at the changes that are currently occurring to us and the planet. Along with these changes come a group of case histories which are not ordinary. These are people who have come to this lifetime with memories which are outside of what would normally be considered "normal". Really, there is nothing particularly strange about these case histories or the individuals whose stories they are, they just reflect the level of change that is, and has been, occurring for several years.

The changes discussed in the last chapter have been eagerly anticipated for quite a number of years and some of our clients have brought aspects of these changes with them in preparation for the time when we will all regain our true potential.

These cases should be seen in this light - they are not really weird, they are just people like you and me who have woken up a little earlier than most of us. Many people will have similar life histories to tell in the future but, for the time being, these cases will be viewed as unusual.

Case Thirty Three
A woman in her forties.

Medical History:
There had been a history of eczema problems since a very young child which flared up at random times but was especially affected by hot weather. Several allergies with grass seeds, cats and several foods, especially processed foods, which could also bring on migraine headaches. Recurring herpes type virus to vagina and lower back. There was a bacterial type infection in the intestines which could make her abdomen swell alarmingly. Severe period pains which were progressively becoming worse. Occasional pains in the hip joints and pelvis.

Family History:
Her father had similar allergies and she seemed to take on the pains of others as her hip/pelvis problems began when her father broke his hip. This was a woman who was actively trying to accelerate her own psychic awareness and take an active part in the changes mentioned in the last chapter. She had recently moved to a new part of the country and had a new man in her life which made her feel very stable and secure. Generally very happy but concerned about her health problems becoming more pronounced.

Our Findings:
She was allergic to herself, or at least her female hormones, especially oestrogen and this brought about many of the other problems.

Her eczema was brought about by the receptor cells of the nerves in her skin being extremely sensitive to the world around her. Some of this problem was brought about by her sensitivity to her own oestrogen which has an important role in skin cells. However, from a chakra viewpoint, the root cause of the eczema was with a first and sixth chakra link. As she was developing her psychic abilities (sixth chakra) it was stimulating the nervous system and as she was a little unsure about her changing abilities, it affected her skin (first chakra).

Her hip problem stemmed from a high degree of empathy with others. There was actually nothing wrong with her hips and pelvis, she had just empathised with her father to a point where she had taken on his pain.

Her stomach problems stemmed from a bacterial infection which flared up periodically in response to her emotional condition (third chakra) and her diet allergies. We suggested a couple of doses of neat vodka for the bacteria which worked extremely well!

Her biggest problem, however, which brought about all of the other problems, was this.

She had lived several lifetimes as a woman but, in this lifetime, she had decided to switch to being a man. At the last minute, she had panicked and overlaid the male gene structures with female as she was more comfortable with the female body form. What this means, in practical terms, is that her whole primary genetic structures were male even though her body form was quite clearly female. As she began to deliberately develop herself in terms of the new energies, her male genetic structure asserted itself more and more.

A major function of these energy changes is to clear out any unwanted past memories (DNA sequences), making our genetic structures as strong as possible. By attempting to accelerate these changes within her body, her primary DNA sequences began to assert themselves, throwing off the overlying female DNA structures. She was progressively becoming more and more allergic to the high levels of oestrogen which her body wanted to naturally produce, whilst her genetic structures were increasingly telling her that it was unnatural. She was literally tearing herself apart from the inside out.

As her wish was to remain female, changing to a male body would bring about its own problems, we could only alter the energy balance within her DNA make up, making the female components the primary sequencing. The male components were then, effectively, switched off. Within a month, her whole system had begun to settle and she had the first "proper" period of her life.

This was not an immediate removal of these symptoms as it took several months for her body to reach a new state of balance. Her eczema still flares up occasionally but as she becomes more confident within herself, the attacks are lessening both in frequency and severity. We also suggested that she did not push herself quite so strongly into the changes of energy as she was overloading her system.

As a note about these current energy changes. As mentioned above, one of the functions of these changes is to clear out any unwanted past memories. Our genetic structures are made up of literally thousands of short sequences of coding information which records everything that we are or have ever been. As these new energies carry out their intended task, they are clearing out our old memories which we no longer need. As this clearance continues, we are actually becoming stronger. This means that in future, once these changes are complete, we will no longer suffer from illness neither will we be subject to the horrendous problems brought about by the pollutants we have filled our environment with as our systems will be strong enough to throw off any outside influence. A world free of illness! A goal well worth striving for.

Case Thirty Four
A woman in her late twenties.

Medical History:
She had been experiencing epileptic type fits since the age of twelve. They came and went a little but were made worse by stress and anxiety and around her menstrual periods. There was a history of very bad headaches over her left eye. There were a number of problems associated with her periods, which were extremely painful, and there was a concern that the uterus lining was not clearing properly leading to blockages within the fallopian tubes. A recent smear test showed abnormal cells to the cervix. Her shoulders had a habit of spontaneously dislocating, especially the left which had been operated on a couple of years previously to stop the problem. The surgery had been largely successful but the steel plate added during the surgery caused her some problems. The right shoulder was now beginning to dislocate more frequently.

Family History:
She came from a close and loving family who tried to help her as much as possible. She had married a few years ago which turned out to be a disaster and was now divorced and living at home with her parents.

Our Findings:
There were lower back problems (first and second chakras - insecurity within her ex marriage) and her right kidney was not functioning very well (first chakra clearance).

The tendons holding the shoulder joints in place were very weak allowing the shoulders to spontaneously dislocate (first chakra - high sense of responsibility).

The left ovary and connected fallopian tube were blocking at each period causing considerable pain and there was an irritation to the cervix with intermittent bleeding (second chakra - sexual relationships).

All of the third chakra organs were badly under functioning. Liver (guilt), gall bladder (anger), spleen (frustration - especially connected to suppressed anger) and there was irritation to the ascending colon (emotional "debris").
The thymus was not working very well and the upper body lymph tissue was badly blocked, especially to the neck (fourth chakra - self love).

The thyroid was under functioning (fifth chakra - sense of being prevented from speaking her truth). The blood oxygenation function of the lungs was functioning very badly which was a major component of her fits (fifth chakra - felt unable to speak her truth, although this also links to the fourth chakra, blood and circulation, connected to the sense of lack of self worth).

The hypothalamus was not functioning very well, disrupting nerve impulses to and from the brain and body (sixth chakra - psychic senses) and the pituitary gland was not working very well disrupting her hormonal balance (sixth chakra but also linked into the primary function of the fourth chakra - the link between the soul and the physical body).

On an energy level, every single chakra was totally depleted and all of the meridians were blocked.

This was a young woman who had come into this life anticipating that most of the current energy changes would be complete and so her energy structures, the energy contained within the chakras, were of the new colours and frequencies. When she reached puberty, and all of her available consciousness attempted to make its final connections to the body, the energetic pathways within the physical body could not tolerate the high levels of energy and she literally blew a fuse. This so disrupted her body that any event in her life had a major impact on the associated chakra and the physical organs became severely disrupted. To a certain extent, it was a miracle that she had survived her life so far. Because she subconsciously knew that she was a little different to the rest of us, she had an enormous sense of responsibility to the world, resulting in the shoulder problems. She also felt that she had to sort out everyone else's problems, to help them through their changes, which added to the sense of responsibility.

The only way to help her was to totally rebuild her chakras and energy structures in a way which allowed her to function in the world as it is. We also had to help her to understand that she had an almost unbelievable psychic potential which was not ready to be used and so she could let go of her sense of responsibility until it was the right time for her to realise her full potential and begin her true work, at some time in the future, when others have undergone their own changes and caught up with her.

Her future role had a very strong link with who she had been in a previous life. The relevant lifetime had been in early Egypt.

What this woman was in ancient Egypt was the principle pyramid builder.

There continues to be a great deal of discussion about how the pyramids were built. In some ways it is very simple, but it does involve a leap of imagination and a temporary suspension of disbelief.

We all have a range of latent psychic abilities, most of which have not been actively used for many centuries. However, there was a time when the whole range of psychic capabilities were used on a day to day basis and one such time was early Egypt.

The method of construction is true for virtually all of the ancient sites, whether in Egypt, South America, Britain, Atlantis, etc. and this was to bring together a group of like minded people who can link together in a single frequency of thought. This collective thought can be a sound, the image of a colour or even a word just as long as all of the members of the group are on an identical thought wave. Once the single resonance has been established, the power of the thought can, literally, move mountains. Or, as in the case of Egypt, pyramids. This woman had the capability of generating the thought and providing the harmonics to fine tune the whole process with the remainder of the group providing the force of energy needed to raise and place the massive blocks of stone. This kind of process is still carried out today in some remote Bhuddist temples in Tibet where huge blocks of stone are placed in position by thought and sound alone.

When this young woman fulfils her potential, it does not mean that she will go on to build new pyramids, but such telekinetic potential can be used, for example, to alter the atomic structure of nuclear waste, rendering it harmless. All is not yet lost!

Case Thirty Five
A boy of sixteen.

Medical History:
About six weeks previously he had begun to rapidly withdraw from the world. There had been a loss of speech and all coordination and balance had been lost. There was a cycle of

fever and high temperatures and calm. Severe headaches to the left side of the head. Complete loss of confidence and he had changed from being a keen music lover to now finding that music disturbed him. Blood tests had been inconclusive and the medical diagnosis was for some kind of glandular fever and the doctors were beginning to insist on a psychiatric evaluation. A cranial osteopath had been consulted and he reported some kind of bio-electrical blockage at the base of the skull which he could not explain.

Family History:
His parents had been going through an acrimonious divorce which took several years to resolve through the courts resulting in severe stress within this boy's life. However, his problems did not seem to stem from his parent's troubles.

Our Findings:
We would describe this young man as being one of the "First Born" of the planet. What we mean by this is fully described in our previous book "The Fool's First Steps", but what it amounted to is this.

Humanity, as we currently are and have been throughout the whole of our 80 000 year history (approximately) have come to this planet from the realms of what we would describe as "The Angels". This means that most of us are, essentially, visitors to our world. We arrived in our purely energetic form and built for ourselves a physical body. This is how humanity began life.

Following the establishment of Atlantis, the need was for a complete human being to be formed. This was achieved by utilising the human "etheric template" that had been developed on Earth and perfected in Atlantis. Into this etheric template, the Creator imbued a full consciousness. This is what we mean by the first born, an individual of this planet with a directly created consciousness. Only 1358 individuals were created in this way and this is what makes this young man very special. This is a full consciousness, a complete human being. This is the state where all of the consciousness is fully integrated into the physical body, where there are thirteen complete spirals to the DNA, where the body has a density approximately one third of what we experience today. It is into this condition that our current energy changes are taking the human race.

A state of fully integrated consciousness is where the higher self is drawn into the physical body and we exist in a state where all of our consciousness, in all of its immensity, can be readily called upon. When you consider that we used to living with a conscious mind which only allows ready access to about 30% of our total consciousness, we are looking at a major shift in understanding (the other 70% constitutes the higher self).

With this young man, he was born into this life with all of these potentials intact. Up until puberty, which he went through very late, he was a "normal" child. When the remainder of his consciousness tried to fully integrate with his physical body, at puberty, he began to see humanity for what it is, largely unchanged from its recent past. With the realisation that he could not yet properly exist within this world, he withdrew.

To a certain extent, his withdrawal from the world is typical of many teenagers, especially in the last ten years or so. These new/old souls have arrived on the planet anticipating that these changes would be in full swing only to find humanity still caught up in the quagmire of the past and very reluctant to let go. As this realisation has dawned, these young adults have been shocked into withdrawing and drug dependency results. This is obviously not true for all teenagers but, for many, it is the sad truth.

As far as this young man was concerned, the only way to help him was to clear the energy pathways within the brain and the body. His cranial osteopath had been quite right, there was a bio-electrical blockage in the neck. This coincided with the hypothalamus which is the "interface" between the physical body and the mind (sixth chakra). By creating a wish to withdraw, the body had manifested a breakdown between the physical world and the world of the consciousness. In removing this blockage, we had to help him, and his mother, understand what his predicament actually was.

He is still not fully functional, to normal standards never mind about his standards, and we suspect that he will not be until the rest of us have let go and began to reach his energy capabilities.

This young man represents who we are and what we should be, let us hope that we match up to his expectations of who we really are.

*****

As we said at the beginning of this book, we have used only genuine case histories from people who have consulted us at our healing practise. This following case is one which some will have difficulty in accepting. We are in the process of change and there are many from outside of our solar system who are here to help us in our change.

The reported incidents involving those we know as "angels" are increasing dramatically and even American and Russian astronauts are reporting seeing "beings" who shadow their craft for a while and then take off at unbelievable speeds. This case history falls into this kind of category. Make of it as you wish but we are convinced that our findings are genuine. To make greater sense of it, see *The Fool's First Steps*.

To quote a well known television programme: "the truth is out there", it is just considerably stranger than fiction.

Case Thirty Six
A woman in her early thirties.

Medical History:
There were no real reported medical symptoms other than this woman felt at the end of her tether trying to understand the world around her and how it interacted with her. She was out of work, retired on medical grounds, because of her experiences.

Family History:
She had been physically abused as a child and this form of abuse had continued for most of her adult life, even from strangers. She had received counselling for these kinds of problems which had helped her but she could not understand why these incidents had occurred since she was not playing the role of the victim. She was a very gentle person who was not aggressive to anyone and yet she found aggression towards her. This form of problem persisted in work and she was in the process of suing her ex employers for harassment at work. The harassment at work had manifested itself as her managers would always be aggressive towards her to the point where even walking down a corridor they would shoulder barge her for no reason. She had tried a number of approaches to try to understand the problem but none had given her any satisfactory conclusions.

Our Findings:
We have to say that we found this woman, although troubled and confused, to be kind, intelligent, considerate, thoughtful and extremely pleasant.

She had been born with all of the new energy structures intact as well as all of the DNA spirals. An almost complete consciousness. However, this was not a "normal" energy pattern. Neither were there any "karmic" memories built into her genetic memory structures. There were thirteen spirals to her DNA but no problem past life memories.

In energy terms, she is an alien. She has no past experience of life on Earth but has come here to assist humanity in its great period of change. Her assistance is offered with love and compassion. Her originating region of the galaxy we know as the Plaiedes.

As a result of her place of origin, everyone she encounters on Earth subconsciously recognises her energy patterns as being different. Most people would not recognise or even understand why they saw her as different but it engendered a response which many humans would resort to - aggression. If something is different and we do not understand it, we react aggressively. This is what had happened to this woman. By being different, most people responded to her presence with aggression. They would not know why they responded in this way, there was just something about her which they felt they had to respond to and the, apparently, most appropriate response was aggression.

As we explained this to her, she burst into tears as, suddenly, her life could be understood. It all made perfect sense to her.We suggested that she disguise herself until the rest of us were grown up enough to deal with and accept the truth. Although her physical body was the same as everyone else, her energy patterns marked her out as being different. To prevent the continuation of the aggression problem, she needed to disguise her amazing energies until such time as the rest of us could properly understand who she was and accept the amazing love she had brought with her to share.

The best way to achieve a disguise, either for aliens or for others who have begun to change their energies and are receiving an aggressive response from those around them, is to use this technique.

Before leaving home or encountering other people who have reacted aggressively towards you, stand still and imagine that you are building a wall around you. This wall needs to be about 2ft (60cm) away from the body and about 2ft (60cm) in thickness.

Start at the level of your feet with the wall being built out of the colour red. You can imagine the wall being constructed in several ways, but the most effective we have found is to either imagine a "doughnut" shape of coloured energy or a concrete block of colour. However you find the best way of imagining this wall, begin with the red of the old first chakra and then build another layer of orange, another layer of yellow, a layer of green, a layer of blue, a layer of indigo and, finally, a layer of violet finishing just above the top of the head. In other words, a wall of the old chakra colours that totally surrounds the body from the feet to the top of the head.

This will effectively disguise your new energies from those you encounter in your day to day life. Once you have built the wall, in your mind, once, all you need to do is to think "chakra wall" and it will be in place. Or, if you are like us and watch science fiction movies, try "shields up", it works just as well. It is an extremely efficient form of psychic defence as well as disguise and can be used in many situations. If, for example, you are visiting a sick friend and always find the visits "draining", you can build the wall before you see your friend and instead of depleting your energies, they will take from the wall, leaving your energies fully intact.

Protection or disguise, the chakra wall is extremely effective and our Plaiedean friend is now living a life less filled with aggression.

As a note about this case history.

Most people will be surprised by our findings and conclusions, some might even throw up their hands in horror at the concept. To put this case into context, remember the first born of the planet, there are only 1358 of these souls in the whole of creation. Everyone else who lives on Earth, as a human, is a visitor from another realm.

True humans are the first born, all of the rest of us are something other. Most come from the realms we know as the angels, the rest from a variety of locations such as the home world of this young woman and this isn't even beginning to look at the Faerie.

But, whilst on that note, there was one day which stands out in our minds as being the perfect example of the reality of the present time. Our first client of the day was a confused and anxious Plaiedean. His problems stemmed from a strong fear of a world he had difficulty understanding. To an alien soul our world can seem pretty alien.

Our second client was someone entirely unique. Within the realms of those beings we know as the faerie, there are a group known as the SidhÇ (pronounced Shee). These are beings of pure energy who are the driving force behind the faerie. The SidhÇ are not currently active on the planet for a variety of reasons and so to find one of their ranks living a human physical lifetime came as something of a surprise. He was equally confused and concerned that humanity's change was very slow in happening as it is preventing the SidhÇ from returning to their rightful place on the planet.

Our third client was what most people would call an angel.

This was a young woman who had difficulty maintaining her hold on the physical world and would spontaneously leave her body without warning. Another result of the lack of change within humanity.

Plaiedean, Sidhé, Angel - not quite a normal day, not even for us.

The reality of the truth really is stranger than fiction.

Chapter Ten

Medical Case Histories

We have called this chapter medical case histories because a percentage of our clients consult us as a result of problems encountered with medical treatment received from the medical profession. A British government study published in mid 1999 gave the statistic that 1.3 million people annually in Britain are hospitalised as a direct result of the medical treatment they have received. These are not people who are on a waiting list but people who have been treated by a medical doctor and have ended up in hospital as a direct result of the treatment they have received.

Our research would indicate that this figure is the tip of the iceberg. Whilst researching for *"Everything You Always Wanted To Know About Your Body But, So Far, Nobody's Been Able To Tell You"*, a number of people gave us their experiences of the medical profession. We also came across many reports in magazines, books and web sites etc. of people's experiences with their doctors. It does not make you overly confident with the medical profession!

One three year study* into the state of medicine in America, the conclusions of which have never been challenged, stated that 300 000 people, in America, are killed each year as a direct result of medical treatment. As the treatments given in Britain are very much the same as in America, it would appear that the same proportion of people suffer a similar fate in Britain although official figures are not available. The word killed was actually used in the summary of the report. [*The study was carried out by an American consumer watchdog organisation headed by Ralph Nader and his 1,500 page report was published in January 1993]

The case histories we have given here are of people who have consulted us and so we have direct experience of the problems they have encountered. Two of the cases, in particular, touched us very deeply and the final outcome of their experiences we consider to be totally unnecessary.

Medical surgery is a haphazard process. The skill of some surgeons is astounding whilst the average surgeon can be extremely lax in their procedures and surgical care. Although the surgery would seem to undo a health problem, the complications resulting from some medical surgery, in our experience, can really be too high a price to pay for the relief of symptoms.

We have not given a chakra diagnosis for these cases as, although they may have brought about the original conditions which warranted the initial visit to their GP, it was as a result of the treatment received from the medical profession that brought them to visit us. Having read this far into this book, the chakra root causes should be self evident.

Given our philosophy and our experiences of working with clients, apart from accident and emergency units, we cannot see any reason for any kind of intrusive medical surgery at all. Whatever the symptoms are, by tracking down the region of your life which is bringing about the symptoms, all illnesses can be undone. A little work on these life problems means that you can cure yourself of anything.

Incidentally, we have also treated many clients who have consulted other complimentary practitioners and, in our experience, no form of complication has arisen. The only problems these clients seem to have encountered from their treatments is that it did not fully remove the symptoms.

Case Thirty Seven
A woman in her fifties.

Medical History:
Some years previously she had undergone a partial hysterectomy that had left her ovaries in place. Since the operation, she had been experiencing a certain amount of pain in the lower abdomen and an ultrasound scan had shown up a large cyst on the left ovary for which further surgery was proposed. She had experienced two periods of major discomfort in the lower abdomen followed by vaginal discharges of a large quantity of very smelly fluid which relieved the pressure. Both of these discharges had occurred shortly after returning from holiday.

Family History:
Her teenage children lived with her following her divorce several years previously. The children were very demanding and she rarely found time for herself. Her only break was her annual holiday and it was following her holidays that the discharges occurred.

Our Findings:
Her lifestyle meant that there were a great many frustrations in her life which she found very difficult to let go of. This situation generated a third chakra (spleen) problem which tended to block up her lower body lymphatic tissue. The surgery she had undergone for the hysterectomy had cut through one of the major lymph channels creating a pocket of isolated lymph tissue that was unable to drain very easily.

Over a period of time, trapped toxins would build up within these isolated lymph nodes producing a massive swelling (up to the size of a grapefruit). It was this swelling that had shown up on the ultrasound scan, not a cyst. When she went off on holiday, she would relax and the abdominal muscles would begin to let go of the trapped lymph fluid. As they could not drain into the spleen because of the surgical scar, they drained into the nearest available channel, which was the vagina, producing the uncomfortable and embarrassing discharge. The channel through to the vagina was through the scars left when the uterus had been removed in her hysterectomy operation. By using some of the techniques described in chapter one, it was possible to reconnect the isolated lymph nodes back into the main drainage channel and the problem is now resolved although she still has to deal with the original causes of her frustration for herself.

Whilst this is an extreme example, we have treated several clients with disrupted lymph channels as a direct result of abdominal surgery. Medical surgeons do seem to have a bad habit of not sewing the bits back together very well.

Case Thirty Eight
A man in his sixties.

Medical History:
He had been diagnosed as suffering from prostate cancer some months prior to coming to see us. He had opted to take medical advice and had undergone radiotherapy and was beginning a course of chemotherapy.

Family History:
He was a very successful businessman who had recently retired. He had a very close and loving family and his prostate problems stemmed from a refusal to take up any kind of creative pursuit (the primary function of the second chakra) despite a great deal of encouragement from his family.

Our homework suggestion to him was to take up pottery lessons as this seemed to be the most appropriate form of expression for him. When he eventually began his classes, following a great deal of resistance on his part, he found that he thoroughly enjoyed them and became the life and soul of the classes. Once he began the classes, his prostate problems went away of their own accord.

Our Findings:
As mentioned above, his prostate problems stemmed from a lack of creativity in his life and despite the fact that he felt as though the problem had been resolved when he took up his pottery classes, he gave in to medical pressure and continued his chemotherapy treatment. Virtually all of the ensuing health problems stemmed from the medical treatment.

The radiotherapy treatment had caused damage to his liver which was then put under considerable strain by the toxicity of the chemotherapy drugs. The constant supply of the drugs kept the liver under pressure and his system began a slow process of collapse.

He was eventually hospitalised and had to be fed through a tube. The reason for this was that his tongue had swollen considerably and he had increasing difficulty in swallowing. We could find no reason for the tongue to swell in this way and we had increasing difficulty in countering this problem or in making him comfortable as the build up of toxic chemicals from the chemotherapy was making a number of his body's systems progressively collapse. He passed away shortly afterwards.

Whilst researching for *Everything You Always Wanted To Know About Your Body*, we came across a report in What Doctors Don't Tell You about one of the chemotherapy drugs, taken by this man, which has the side effect of making the saliva glands under the tongue swell, causing the tongue to block the throat, creating difficulties in swallowing and, eventually, breathing.

Given these side effects are not uncommon, surely the medical profession need to keep a closer eye on patients in their care and drug treatments stopped when such serious complications arise.

At a time when the world was preparing itself to go to war, the British parliament found time to pass into law The 1939 Cancer Act. This law specifically prohibits the publication, by any means, of the complimentary treatments available for cancer.

There are a great many complementary treatments, dating back many hundreds of years, many of which have been proven to work without side effects. We cannot tell you any specifics about these treatments as we would be breaking the law.

Given Britain has one of the worst records on cancer treatments in the world (the government's own words), is it not time that this ridiculous law was repealed and there was free and open discussion and evaluation of all of the cancer treatments available?

Case Thirty Nine
A woman in her thirties.

Medical History:
Following the birth of her second child she had a contraceptive coil fitted. Shortly afterwards she became pregnant again, despite the coil, which resulted in the birth of her third child. She felt as though the coil had become displaced but her doctors told her that was impossible and that it must have fallen out without her noticing!

Following the birth, she had a sterilisation operation. The sterilisation did not go very well and she had recurring abdominal problems which were left largely untreated despite numerous visits to her GP. Ten years after the sterilisation, she became pregnant again resulting in a miscarriage. There followed a major infection in the uterus resulting in a full hysterectomy. Whilst carrying out the hysterectomy, the surgeons found that the coil had displaced itself, probably shortly after being fitted, and had ripped through the intestines embedding itself in the base of the spine. The discharge from the damaged intestines had built up within the uterus and resulted in the infection.

For a number of years she had tolerated major pain in her lower back, hip and thighs which became so severe at times that she would collapse from the pain. Her doctors told her that there was nothing wrong and the pain was her imagination. She was attempting to sue her area health authority over this series of blunders but she could not find a doctor who would give evidence against another doctor nor could she find a solicitor prepared to take on the medical profession.

Our Findings:
The internal damage caused by the coil displacing was considerable and whilst the hysterectomy surgery had helped to correct many of the problems, one major one remained. When it had embedded itself into the spine, the coil had partially severed the sciatic nerve to the left hip and leg. This meant that there was constant pain in these regions and, if she became tired or stressed, the muscles of the lower back would lock and she would collapse from the resulting pain caused by the additional pressure on this nerve.

We managed to repair much of the nerve damage and suggested that she take a course of potassium supplements to help strengthen the nerve tissue. We also suggested that she treat herself to a series of aromatherapy massages to help ease all of the muscle stresses in the lower back and abdomen. We think it would be a really good idea if doctors actually paid attention to what their patients have to say to them about their conditions, it might actually save them many years of severe pain and trauma.

Case Forty
A man in his sixties.

Medical History:
About twenty years ago he had a bypass operation where they had taken an artery from his left leg to build the bypass in his chest and he had minor leg problems since. He had a history of hip problems which resulted in a diagnosis of the right leg being shorter than the left and, about ten years before coming to see us, he had a hip replacement operation to the left hand side.

On waking from the operation, he found his leg in traction as they had accidentally broken his femur (thigh bone) in three places. The hip replacement had also failed and he underwent a new replacement operation six months later. On waking from the second operation, he found he was in traction again as they had accidentally broken the femur in a further two places and the bone was now held together by a steel plate.

Since the second operation, he had constant trouble with the left hip and he was unable to walk for more than 200 yards (200 metres) before the calf muscles of the left leg became rigid and he could no longer walk. After waiting for two or three minutes, the muscles would ease and he could walk a further 200 yards before the muscles would lock again. The medical investigation into the problem showed that there was a plug of material in the blood vessels of his calf and he had undergone two angioplastys but without success.

An angioplasty is where a blood vessel is opened and a balloon like device inserted. When the balloon is inflated, it pushes a blockage further down the blood vessel in the hope that by dislodging the blockage, the body will dispose of it naturally. All that these angioplastys had done for this man was to push the blockage into a smaller blood vessel and the medical prognosis was that the leg would need to be amputated below the knee.

Our Findings:
We certainly confirmed that there was a plug of material in the blood vessels of the calf which was causing an intermittent blockage of one of the small blood vessels.

When he was at rest, the plug would ease slightly and there would be a restricted blood flow into the calf muscles. However, once he began to walk, the extra blood pressure brought about by the movement, pushed the plug further into the blood vessel and blood flow to the muscles would virtually cease causing the muscles to lock. Once he stopped walking, the pressure would ease, the blood begin to flow again and the muscles relax.

The plug of material turned out to be a piece of bone marrow dislodged and released into the blood vessels of the leg when the surgeons accidentally broke the femur during his hip replacement operations.

Case Forty One
A woman in her seventies.

Medical History:
There had been a history of period problems which had resulted in her undergoing a complete hysterectomy for uterine and ovarian cancer about fifteen years previously. The treatment she received was a little unusual. She had twenty

three separate dosages of radiation and five balls of irradiated stainless steel had been sewn into her abdomen and she was placed in an isolation ward for three days before the balls were removed - can you believe this?

There had been a history of lower back problems for several years for which she had consulted an osteopath and the medical diagnosis was that she had arthritis in the lower spine. She had a slight stroke about two years previously which had left her with a slight restriction in movement to her left side. There was almost constant pain to her left hip and knee which was becoming progressively worse. She was urine incontinent and had been for a number of years.

Our Findings:
The radiation treatment, but in particular, the irradiated stainless steel balls, had destroyed much of the nerve tissue within the abdomen.

All of the nerves connected to and surrounding the bladder had been eaten away by the radiation and she could neither feel nor control the flow of urine. The sciatic nerve had been severely damaged by the radiation, particularly to the left side, and this resulted in her pain in the left hip and left knee. As she was becoming older and the tissues did not regenerate so readily, the damage was becoming worse which resulted in the increase in the pain. Such extensive damage to one region of her nervous system had put such a strain on the rest of her nervous system that the stroke had resulted. The radiation had also eaten away much of the bone structure of the upper pelvis and the lower spine resulting in the medical diagnosis of arthritis although it was, in reality, more a case of severe bone loss.

How can the medical profession treat a degenerative illness such as cancer with a substance (radiation) that causes cancer in healthy people and not expect there to be long term side effects? - always assuming you have survived the treatment for enough time to be considered long term. Sewing irradiated metal into the abdomen for three days is really beyond belief!

Case Forty Two
A woman in her late eighties.

Medical History:
This was a woman who had always been very fit and active, took life as it came and very rarely complained.

About eight years previously she had suffered a major hernia in the lower abdomen. An operation had ensued which had gone very wrong. The surgery was repeated but the stitches had turned septic and she had a history of recurring infections since. She was in constant pain and her abdomen had progressively swollen since the operation and her lower back was now affected. The situation had become so bad that she was bed ridden, much to her frustration. Her GP seemed reluctant to treat her further and her surgeon had refused to carry out investigative surgery on the grounds that she was too weak and old and might not survive the surgery.

Our Findings:
The whole of her abdomen was a mess. The surgical scars, especially at a deep level, were badly infected and the muscles had not been put back into place properly. However, the reason for her problems were that several items from the surgery had been left in place.

There was a fabric swab across the whole width of the abdominal cavity which was adhering to the intestines. Every time she moved the intestines would pull at the swab and severe pain would result. Attached to the swab was a length of plastic tube which had been inserted as a drain during the second operation. The end of the tube was embedded in the muscles of the abdomen which had closed around it. Every movement pulled on the tube and wrenched it away from the muscles adding to the severe pain in the abdomen. The infection in the abdominal cavity was becoming worse and causing the swelling.

We made her as comfortable as possible and helped with the infection. Whilst we can work with most conditions within the body, there is very little we can do with artificial material. If it is naturally occurring, we can read and find its energy frequency and, usually, do something to help. Where there are problems brought about by man made materials, as in this case, the energy frequencies of such material are almost impossible to work with and so, regrettably, there was very little we could do to help this poor woman.

Case Forty Three
A man in his seventies.

Medical History:
This was a man who was extremely fit and active with many hobbies, especially walking, cooking and eating. There had been spinal problems following an accident in his teenage years but he had not had any back problems since.

About four years previously he had passed congealed blood from his bladder for a couple of days and he had consulted his GP. On examination, his GP told him that he had haemorrhoids but that there were other problems and made him an appointment to see a consultant. He was given an endoscope inspection of the bladder, through his penis, and told that he had a polyp growth. The polyp was removed by endoscope and an appointment made for six months time. For the next four years, he visited the consultant every six months for an endoscope inspection with a new polyp growth being removed each time. Each polyp was sent for analysis for cancer and each time the results came back inconclusive. Six months prior to coming to see us, an unusually large polyp had been removed and the consultant decided to proceed with full cancer treatment "just in case". The consultant stated that the treatment would make him feel woozy for three weeks but that after this period "he would be as right as rain".

Our findings:
We saw this man four times and feel that we should present his case as a diary of each visit.

First Visit.
The treatment had begun two months previously where he had been given a dose of radiation through the right hip and was now on a course of chemotherapy. He was very weak and had virtually no appetite. When he did eat, within half an hour a pain began in the region of the kidneys which would last for three hours. The pain had become so intense that he was on three doses of morphine per day. The same problem occurred whether he ate solid food or was put on a food tube by the hospital. Anything which required digesting caused the problem. Following the initial radiotherapy, he had been given an x-ray which required a radioactive injection.

Our Findings:
The body tells a story, if you know how to ask, and gives up its secrets and memories quite readily. As far as we could read the response we received, there had never been cancer in the bladder, or anywhere else, before the treatment was given.

There was severe radioactive damage to the whole of the abdominal cavity and the right pelvis bone structure was beginning to disintegrate with extensive bone cancer from the radiation. The intestines were extremely badly damaged by the radiation as were the liver and the spleen. The liver was also being further damaged by the cocktail of chemicals from the chemotherapy. There had been a history, over many years, of a slight weakness within the left lung and this was being aggravated by a build up of radiation borne by the blood circulation.

Second Visit - one week later.
His eating had become more comfortable and he was able to keep more food down. He was very constipated but that was improving and he did not retch on eating quite so often. His lower back, left hip and right leg were causing him increasing pain.

Since his last visit to us he had returned to the hospital where they had given him a CAT scan which also involved an iodine drink to make the cells fluoresce under the scanner and he had been given an endoscope inspection of the throat and small intestines through his mouth.

Our Findings:
The iodine drink was reacting strongly with the numerous other chemicals in his body and the radiation was causing the muscles of the lower back to go into violent spasms trapping the right sciatic nerve and causing the increasing pain in his right hip and leg. The endoscope inspection had scratched the oesophagus, stomach and small intestines in several places, each of which contained a small pool of radioactive chemicals and were turning cancerous. There were huge radiation and chemical residues in the liver and spleen making them virtually stop working. The function of the pancreas had virtually ceased on every level and the left lung was becoming worse.

Third Visit - one week later.
There had been some further improvement in his eating but the back pain was worse.

Our Findings:
The liver, spleen and pancreas functions were beginning to improve and there was a little more comfort in the intestines. The chemicals and radiation were still causing the muscle spasms in the lower back and the right hip bone structure was beginning to disintegrate from the bone cancer.

Fourth Visit - three weeks later.
He had spent the past couple of weeks in a hospice where his chemotherapy treatment was continuing. Most of his symptoms had returned and his skin and eyes were now bright yellow in colour. His stools were white and his urine was dark brown.

Our Findings:
We "scanned" through the whole of his body and this is what we found.

The pituitary gland was not functioning, totally disrupting the whole of the body's hormone balance. The thyroid was in a state of collapse mainly due to the iodine drink for the CAT scan. The cells of the oesophagus were disintegrating and the stomach lining was not functioning. The left lung was now cancerous. The liver was cancerous and beginning to disintegrate and the spleen was in a state of collapse. The pancreas was just about functioning although the radiation and chemical residue were preventing it from producing its necessary hormones. The right hip and pelvis were in collapse and the lower back muscles were in permanent spasm. Virtually every single cell in his body was in a state of collapse and turning cancerous.

Two weeks later his wife telephoned us to say that he had passed away.

Here we had a vital man who enjoyed life and all that it has to offer.

Polyp growths can be successfully treated by a course of a single Biochemic Tissue Salt. When will the medical profession finally acknowledge that treating someone with cancer with a cancer forming substance (radiation) does not work and only causes further problems. In our experience, virtually all cases of secondary tumours are caused by the radiotherapy. Those who have survived current cancer treatment have done so despite the treatment, not because of it.

Chemotherapy is based upon First World War mustard gas. All of the chemical compounds (drugs) produced since chemotherapy was first introduced act in the same way. Into a body whose immune system is fighting for the body's survival, is added a cocktail of chemicals so destructive that they cannot be given to people who are well as they will kill you, and the body is expected to cope and recover.

There is no logic in this, only a barbaric and wanton destruction.

In our experience, if you receive no treatment whatsoever for cancer, you will live considerably longer and have a better quality of life than if you go down the medical route.

We are all capable of curing ourselves. We just have to remember that we have a soul who tries to talk to us through our bodies. Once we begin to listen, the body responds and all illnesses melt away.

Perfect health is achievable, we just need to listen.

Chapter Eleven

Conclusions

All of the case histories given in this book are about people who have taken a wrong step in their lives and an illness has resulted. What these case histories illustrate is how to read the symptoms of an illness and how to relate it back to the chakra or chakras that connect with those particular regions of the body. Hopefully, what you should have realised is that no illness is necessary or, once an illness has begun, you have it within your own power to bring yourself back to full health. All that is required is a little thought and a small change within the way in which you live your life.

It really is as simple as that - honest!

If you do not believe us, here's a case history which perfectly illustrates the point.

Case Forty Four

A woman in her late eighties.

Medical History:
She could not think of any particular symptoms but would like us to check her over.

Family History:
She lived on her own on a state pension. Her husband had died some years before and she had grown up children.

Our Findings:
Nothing.

She was in perfect health with all of her organs intact and fully functioning.

This was a woman who turned up wearing what most people would describe as "hippy" clothes with her hair dyed bright orange. Most people would consider her to be slightly eccentric but what her attitude really meant was that she had found the right balance for her life. If someone needed help, she was more than ready and willing to supply it but she never forgot herself. For the whole of her life she had lived within this balance. She had brought up her children, kept home for her husband and maintained a wide circle of friends and family, whenever problems arose she would deal with them to the best of her abilities, she spoke her truth and treated other people in the way in which she expected to be treated herself - with honesty and understanding.

Now that she was on her own she visited friends, went to concerts, took short holidays either by herself or with friends and found enjoyment in everything that she did. In many respects, a perfect way of life, a perfect balance and her physical body reflected that. She shone with that inner light that only comes from being yourself.
A lovely woman!

This case history illustrates perfectly how all of our lives should be - in balance. We do not have to become selfish. We do not need to neglect or ignore others. All that we need to do is to be ourselves, express our true feelings and deal with life as it comes.

This is not a simplistic approach to health, but a view based upon twenty years of working with people and observing the patterns of energy brought about by their behaviour. If the

165

patterns are clean and clear, like the woman above, perfect health will be maintained. If we take a wrong step, go against the wishes of the soul, we disrupt those patterns and little swirls begin to appear in our energy structures. If these swirls are allowed to remain in place, the energies of one of the organs begins to become disrupted and the body's functions begin to slow. The body does everything possible to correct this disruption but if we hold the patterns of energy displacement in place, the body cannot function at its normal efficiency and an illness arises. If we correct the energy disruption and bring the energy patterns back to their correct balance, the body will repair itself and the symptoms of illness, no matter how serious, will disappear.

This is the process by which illness arises and how the body can and will repair itself.

Everything that we are is energy and when we are born, all of the body's energies are in balance. If we maintain that balance we have perfect health. If we do not, we fall ill.

Good health is not good luck, it is finding the right balance in life.

What the case above illustrates is that no matter what we do in life as long as we maintain the balance between our needs and serving the needs of others, our bodies will maintain its health and strength. The spine, the joints and all of the organs will continue functioning normally for as long as we let them. The longest recorded lifetime was 220 years - if we all lived our lives in balance, be ourselves, we all could live that long.

Our world is not an easy place to be healthy in. Every so called scientific advance has added potential stresses to our lives and dangers within our work place, added chemicals to our foods and into our homes. All of these chemicals are poisons. However, if we maintain the correct balance within our lives, all of these potential poisons will have no harmful affect as our systems will be strong enough to throw off any outside influence, no matter how powerful their potential effects are. If we do not find that balance illnesses can arise and we can allow the world around us to cause us other, sometimes quite serious, problems. These problems can arise at any age but it is the young who are most susceptible to such outside influences as this last case history illustrates.

Case Forty Five
A young woman of sixteen.

Medical History:
She had a history of problems with her leg muscles for a number of years. There had been several childhood illnesses for which she had been prescribed numerous dosages of antibiotics. About a year ago she had a bad skin rash for which she had been prescribed steroid tablets. Three months before coming to see us she had noticed some changes in her system which had been diagnosed very recently as diabetes.

Family History:
Her parents were very concerned and loving but also very busy in their working lives but they had always striven to provide well cooked wholesome food at home. This young woman had also been brought up on large quantities of fruit squash drinks and fizzy drinks. Also, given the pressure on young women to conform to a particular body form, she had dieted at several times during her life and concentrated on eating mainly low fat foods as well as the fast food diet of many young people.

Our Findings:
Like so many children of her age, she had been born with most of the new energy structures intact (see chapter eight).

This made her very sensitive to the world around her. She was very gentle and considerate of others and also quite shy. This approach to life led, along with her very sensitive energies, to a weakening of several of her chakras.

The first chakra was weakened by her shyness which mainly arose from her arriving into a world which was not quite as far down the energy change as anticipated. This led to her feeling quite insecure within herself leading to some of the muscle problems and the skin rash.

The third chakra was weakened for similar reasons to those of the first chakra and this had put a slight weakness into several of the abdominal organs.

The fourth chakra had been weakened by her wish to help others to the detriment of herself.

The fifth chakra was not operating at full function as she felt that, on many occasions, she could not express herself fully for risk of upsetting someone else.

With these chakra weaknesses in place, other, outside influences, began to take hold.

As we "scanned" her body, it became obvious that there were other problems in addition to those medically diagnosed, all of which were brought about by her food and lifestyle damaging the organs weakened by the depletion of the energies to the various chakras.

Diabetes is an illness brought about by a breakdown in communication between the pancreas and the liver (see chapter six). In this particular case, the liver function had been weakened by her being fearful of many of the situations she encountered in life and this weakness had been made considerably worse by damage caused by the antibiotics and particularly the steroids. The pancreas (emotional force) was a little weak but the cause of the diabetes was that the artificial sweeteners (saccharine and particularly aspartame) in the soft drinks, especially the fizzy ones, were blocking the signals between the pancreas and the liver leading to the liver not producing the correct levels of insulin. This is a known potential side effect of aspartame, see the following chapters for more about this. Although there was a weakness within the organs concerned, the diabetes was caused directly by the artificial sweeteners found in soft drinks.

The cause of her muscle problems were also quite interesting. The fifth chakra controls the function of the thyroid and parathyroid glands in the neck. The thyroid controls body's metabolism whilst the parathyroid controls the levels of calcium within the blood and bones. Her sense of being prevented from speaking "her truth" as much as she would like led to a slight problem with the parathyroid. However, soft, fizzy drinks contain a high level of phosphorous. Phosphorous, in high concentrations, is known to strip the body of calcium. It does this by the phosphorous atoms bonding with calcium atoms, a combination which the body does not recognise, and so the mixture is disposed of through the urine. What this means in practical terms is that with the parathyroid not functioning at full strength and maintaining a correct calcium balance throughout the body, the calcium that should have been made use of to make the muscles work correctly was being stripped by the phosphorous leading to weaknesses in all of her muscles but particularly the legs. The parathyroid, in attempting to do its job properly, made up this loss by taking calcium from the bones and this led to this sixteen year old young woman having osteoporosis (over 25% bone loss) in her neck and upper spine.

In addition to these problems, we found that there were early signs of heart disease brought about by a constant diet of low fat processed foods but particularly margarine (see the next chapter).

Although there were chakra weaknesses brought about by the way in which this young woman interacted with the world around her, the damage to her body was caused by the substances found in her diet. The chemicals in processed foods and soft drinks do not do the body any good. Add to this the potential problems of microwaving these foods and we end up with a situation where the body is stripped of its essential components with no supply of the raw materials from which to build replacements.

As most of her originating chakra weaknesses arose from a lack of self confidence, our suggestions to this young woman were to take assertiveness classes or, perhaps, a martial art or even join a drama company to help build her self esteem and confidence, and, most importantly of all, change to an organic diet without soft, fizzy drinks or hydrogenated margarines.

Chapter Twelve
Personal Comments

The case histories detailed in this book have been provided to help understand the workings of the body and how our health is affected by the way in which we live our lives. If we live our lives honestly, openly and true to ourselves, we escape illness. If we try to mould ourselves to the wants and expectations of others, we begin to weaken the soul's links with the physical and illness results.

Unfortunately, being human means that we are subject to all of the frailties that this condition brings and we have become used to ignoring the promptings of the soul with the inevitable consequence of generating weaknesses within the energies of the body. Add to this the polluted conditions in which we live our lives and the physical body is subjected to enormous stresses and strains and many illnesses result.

In this chapter, we would like to pass on some of our findings on these types of illnesses but also some of the research that is being carried out into the additives placed into our food, the chemicals in the environment and the propaganda, self interest and advertising that masquerades as science.

The vast majority of the goods we purchase are promoted in advertising campaigns which are designed to make us buy a product. All that the manufacturer is interested in is selling their products and making a profit. This is the purpose of advertising, to make us buy one manufacturer's product as opposed to another's and the advertising will be as dishonest as the manufacturer can get away with. Very few manufacturers have the consumer's interests in mind when they market a product.

These techniques produce an extremely distorted view of the world we live in as advertising slogans are presented as facts and, very often, the facts are apparently derived from a "scientific" basis. The latest range of advertising campaigns include the words "clinically tested", "in clinical trials", "according to experts", and many more similar claims, all usually mean that the companies have carried out trials using their own staff who have some kind of medical or scientific qualifications and it is the claims made by these company employees which are presented as "expert" evidence.

This kind of problem has now become so misleading and the companies so determined to make their product appear better than those of their competitors that very little independent scientific evidence actually sees the light of day. When genuine research is carried out, the "evidence" presented by these manufacturing and marketing companies is very often shown to be massively flawed. The power of these companies as advertisers means that most of these independent studies are not reported in the newspapers as they could lose their advertising revenues and there have even been instances where court injunctions have been taken out to prevent the publication of independent studies at all.

Even government bodies can be fooled. The American Food and Drug Administration (the FDA), held up by most western governments as being the best regulatory body in the world, has been misled by some companies into passing products as safe for human consumption only to find that the evidence presented by the companies is fundamentally flawed, sometimes, deliberate fraud has been proven, and these were the cases that were found out.

172

The multinational, or transnational, companies are now so rich that their profits can be in excess of the gross national product of some countries. This financial power can mean that they can influence government policy in virtually any country they care to target.

In the Autumn of 1999, a conference of many of the heads of the major multinationals called for the setting up of a European version of the American FDA. Their stated reasons for wanting such a Europe wide body was so that they would only have to have their products approved by one body instead of the approval bodies of each government as the case is now. If such a European body was established it would mean that we would have no say in the activities of these multinational companies. By the word "we" we mean individuals or the governments of individual countries in Europe. These proposals are currently backed by The World Trade Organisation and the European Commission.

Genetically Modified Crops give us the perfect example of the kinds of problems a European approving body could bring about.

As things stand at the moment in Britain, if a biotech company wants to begin growing GM trial crops in order to find out what impact they would have on the environment, they have to go through a number of processes before any trial is allowed. Just why they need to have these trials is very suspect as trials have already been held in America and other countries prior to coming to Britain and all of the information they need, or could want, about these crops they already know from these other trials.

The vetting process in Britain is far from perfect but at least it is something. These companies will begin by citing the results of trials carried out in America and approved by the American FDA. The British government has their own scientific advisors who study the evidence presented and decide whether to grant these companies licenses to grow such crops. There is also a small degree of public consultation about the issue and decisions based upon the evidence and views presented.

Under the new proposals, the EU approving body is approached and the approvals from the FDA presented. If all of the proposals made by the multinationals are adopted, no consultations take place but a blanket approval given to the trials on a European wide basis based upon the documents approved by the American FDA. No individual government is involved and none of the environmental pressure groups are involved. If the FDA has approved a product for trial then the European body must also accept the product for trial. Nobody else has a say in the decision making process.

This is the multinationals' ultimate dream and one which, unfortunately, the European Commission seems to be seriously considering.

Whilst on the subject of multinationals and profit, here is something to consider.

In order for a company to grow it must make a profit. That profit must increase annually in order to provide constant growth. This is the ideal of every company, increasing profit, increasing share of the market and an increasing work force. We are used to this model of how a company should function and expand, most people work for companies who hold this kind of philosophy.

In order for there to be an increase in company expansion, there must be an increase in the number of goods manufactured by the company. The goods are marketed and people persuaded to buy, that's us, the consumers. The company ideal given above, company growth year on year, can only be achieved by increasing the number of goods and products that are manufactured each year.

We live on a lump of rock floating in space. That is all we have, just our lump of rock. We live on a world of finite resources. How can we increase the number of products we manufacture year on year when our planet does not have any other raw materials to plunder? It is time to rethink our philosophies, understand that our planet is all that we have and start to treat the Earth as though we are actually staying.

In a world of finite resources, how can there be constant year on year growth?

Microwave Cooking
Whilst on the subject of how these companies operate, here's a précis of a report written by Sheri Nakken published in *Nexus Magazine* in February/March 1999.

A Swiss scientist called Hans Hertel and a colleague, Bernard H Blanc, of the Swiss Federal Institute of Technology and the University Institute for Biochemistry, carried out a study into the effects of microwaved foods on the human body by feeding microwaved foods to a group of volunteers and measuring any physiological changes.

"The conclusion was clear: microwave cooking changed the nutrients so that changes took place in the participant's blood. These were not healthy changes but were changes that could cause deterioration in the human systems........indicating that food cooked in microwave ovens could pose a greater risk to health than food cooked by conventional means".

The research seemed to show significant changes in the blood of the volunteers who consumed foods cooked in microwave ovens. These changes included a decrease in the ability of blood cells to carry oxygen, an unhealthy change in the proportions of good and bad cholesterol and the reduction in the life span of white blood cells (the body's defence mechanism). All of this adds up to a situation where illnesses of a serious nature could arise.

Additionally, there was a high significant association between the amount of microwave energy in the test foods and this type of energy found in the blood. In other words, the tests seemed to show that the body could hold microwave energy within its cells and this kind of energy can produce cancer type effects on the blood. This led the scientists to the conclusion that such technically derived energies may be "passed along to man inductively via consumption of microwaved food".

[After reading this report, we wondered could this be the reason for the dramatic increase in the incidence of leukaemia?]

When the researchers attempted to publish their findings, the Swiss Association of Manufacturers and Suppliers of Household Appliances and the Swiss Association of Dealers in Electroapparatus for Household and Industry (known as the FEA) brought separate court actions against the scientists to prevent the publication of their report. A court "gagging" order was issued and the report was prevented from being published.

In March 1993, the court handed down this decision based upon the complaint of the FEA: "consideration 1. Request from the plaintiff (FEA) to prohibit the defendant (Dr Hans Hertel) from declaring that food produced in the microwave oven shall be dangerous to health and lead to changes in the blood of consumers, giving reference to pathologic troubles as also indicative for the beginning of a cancerous process.

The defendant shall be prohibited from repeating such a statement in publications and in public talks by punishment laid down in the law......"

However, the scientists were convinced of their findings and took the issue to the Court of Human Rights in Strasbourg. In 1998 the Strassbourg court ruled that the "gag order" issued by the Swiss courts prohibiting the publication of a report stating that microwave ovens are dangerous to health, was contrary to freedom of expression.

The court went further to state that "This decision is to put an end to judicial censorship of persons drawing attention to the health hazards of certain products".

Unfortunately, neither this ruling nor the original research findings on the dangers of microwaved foods have been widely reported. The advertising revenue from companies manufacturing and promoting the use of microwaved ovens for home cooking is very high and if it became publicly known that there could be allegedly potential dangers to health from cooking food in this way, the revenue would cease.

GM Crops
We, people, are beginning to win the war against this insidious threat. Most supermarkets have now banned GM ingredients in their own brand products and there is a huge growth in the sale of organic crops. Despite this, there is still one area where the multinational biotech companies are still winning the propaganda war and this is with crop trials.

Whilst the majority of people do not like the thought of their food being genetically modified, there does seem to be a large number of people who support field trials of these crops although a recent survey showed that even though crop trials are supported, even those who do support them do not want trials to take place near their homes.

What is not generally realised is the way in which the genetic modification process works. Most people seem to think that genetic material is taken from one organism and somehow precisely injected directly into another with no risk of the genetic material spreading. This really is not the case.

Genetic material is transferred from one organism to another by the use of "vectors". Vectors are other organisms such as viruses or bacteria. The most commonly used is the E.coli bacteria but even the AIDS virus has been used as a vector. The desired gene is removed from one organism, placed into a bacteria and the bacteria allowed to reproduce by the million. The bacteria are then introduced into the seeds of the target plant with the hope that the bacteria will infect the seeds in sufficient numbers to invade the seed cell structures and deposit the new gene into the seed's DNA. These seeds are then planted and tested to see if they contain the transferred genetic material. Those that do are replanted and a new form of life is introduced into the world.

However, these vectors are still active in the new plants and the vector transfers itself into the soil around the plant. Bacteria are everywhere on the planet and many live readily in soil. Laboratory tests show that the vectors can remain active in the soil for up to two years, transferring their genetic loads into any other plant planted in the same soil or soil outside of the laboratory when it is disposed of. What field trials have shown is that the vectors can remain active in the ground for at least one year after the original GM crop has been harvested. This means that the vectors will transfer their genetic material into whatever crop is planted in the same soil the following year. This is why one supermarket chain has banned any crop grown in soil that has had a GM crop grown in it.

Vectors have been designed to work with specific types of crops but, the latest vectors, themselves genetically modified for the purpose, can cross any species. This means that once these organisms are present in the soil or the plant, anything coming into contact with them is at risk of being invaded by the genetic material they carry - including people.

The dangerousness of these organisms cannot be stressed too highly. They have the potential to wipe out all life on the planet by endlessly mixing genetic material from any species with any other species leading to a complete breakdown of all forms of life - total genetic meltdown. If these new vectors are released, and there is indications that they could be released as early as 2001, the only life remaining on the planet in a maximum of ten years would possibly be some slime covering exposed rocks - if the slime can survive.

There is no safe minimum for these vector organisms in the environment.

Heart Disease
With the British government announcing a major drive to eradicate heart disease in 1999, we thought it would be a good time to share our findings on what we consider to be the main cause of the astronomical rise of this disease as the major killer in the western world since the beginning of this century. The whole problem centres around cholesterol. Cholesterol is a substance produced by the body to provide raw materials for the immune system and other essential bodily functions. We cannot survive without cholesterol. Healthy cholesterol is known as HDL cholesterol. HDL Cholesterol is manufactured from fats in our diet. The only sources are saturated fats. These are found in meat, butter, whole milk, etc., or mono - unsaturated fats such as olive oil, palm oil, soya oil, etc. Good, healthy cholesterol cannot be manufactured by the body from any other source.

Since the beginning of this century, we have been inundated with advertising campaigns by the vegetable oil and margarine companies informing us that cholesterol is a killer and we must do everything possible to reduce our saturated fat intake by eating margarine, low fat spreads and vegetable oils. These products are manufactured from vegetable sources. When vegetables are processed into oils, they produce a substance called polyunsaturated fats. This is what the expression means, polyunsaturated fats are high in vegetable oil. To turn the oils into cooking oils or margarine like substances, these polyunsaturated fats have to be heated or hydrogenated, or both, to be usable. Hydrogenation is a process where the oils are bombarded with hydrogen atoms to straighten the molecular chains found in vegetable oils. The molecular structure of vegetable oils prevents them from hardening at room temperature so the molecules need to be straightened to make margarine solid. The process is random and some of the hydrogen atoms that do not "pair" remain within the vegetable oil. Nature does not like unpaired atoms and so, when the margarine is eaten, these unpaired atoms search through the body to find an atom they can pair with. If they cannot find one, they are capable of removing atoms from bodily tissues creating another unpaired atom in the process. These unpaired atoms are called free radicals and can cause irreparable damage within the body.

The hydrogenation process makes the oils unstable and produce a vast array of free radicals which scavenge through the body wreaking havoc and considerable damage as they go. In addition, the body cannot digest or absorb these types of fats and calls upon the immune system to heal the damage caused. As the immune system is put under strain, the body draws upon its store of cholesterol to manufacture new immune system components.

So far, it doesn't sound too bad. We are not taking in heavy fats and the body's immune system deals with the free radical damage. But. HDL cholesterol, needed to replenish the immune system, can only be manufactured from saturated fats. If the body is not taking in these types of fats, it does not receive a fresh supply of the raw materials needed to replenish the immune system. When this occurs, the body searches around for other, similar, substances from which it might be able to manufacture cholesterol. If it only finds polyunsaturated fats, it attempts to use them. When this situation occurs, the body cannot synthesise cholesterol correctly as the fats lack the major important ingredients and, instead, produces LDL cholesterol. This type of cholesterol does not benefit the body. It cannot be used by the immune system nor any other bodily system as it will not form the correct chemical chains. Because of this, the LDL cholesterol begins to break apart within the body releasing a vast number of free radicals and massive damage results, especially to the major blood vessels and heart tissues. Result? Heart disease.

It isn't too much cholesterol that kills you, it is too much margarine, low fat spreads, low fat foods and processed foods. The problem is made considerably worse if you have had a hysterectomy. Following menopause, the uterus produces a hormone called prostacyclin which actively guards a woman against heart disease. The uterus is not the only organ that produces this hormone but it is a major source post menopause. If you have had a hysterectomy and are on a low fat diet, heart disease is virtually guaranteed.

Cholesterol is a substance which the body needs. There are many false impressions about this substance, most of which have been derived from advertising hype or "medical" reports paid for by margarine companies. The truth, borne out by independent medical research, is that there is no such thing as too much cholesterol in your system. That is HDL cholesterol. However, too little cholesterol can cause paranoia, mood swings, aggression and several other similar symptoms. Before taking the advertising seriously, try and read up on the facts - the two are not the same.

Asthma

One of the main scourges of the twentieth century is the incidence of asthma. In adults, we are looking at a fifth chakra problem, aggravated by the various pollutants we breathe in on a daily basis. With children, there are other causes.

We touched on one reason for childhood asthma in chapter seven with the past life link. This really is a serious problem and one which does account for a large number of such cases. But, quite clearly, there are other causes which can either generate asthma symptoms by themselves or further add to the problem already established by genetic memory.

One major cause is vaccination, particularly from the diphtheria vaccine.

In our experience, most vaccines create many of the problems they were designed to prevent. We have come across many reports of the damage caused by the measles vaccine. For example, in a major outbreak of the illness in America a few years ago, the children who had been vaccinated all came down with measles, many with the most virulent form. Those with the least dangerous form, or did not contract the disease at all, had not been vaccinated (source WDDTY).

The problem with vaccines is that they introduce a small amount of a virus into the body in the hope that the body's own immune system will develop antibodies to build up a resistance to the disease if it is encountered in later years. In theory, this should work on a similar basis as the first principle of homeopathy, like cures like. Unfortunately, the vaccination is given to new born babies who do not have a functioning immune system and the virus then has free reign to wreak havoc as it will.

It does not matter the vaccine is made from a live virus or a dead virus, the infants body still has to cope with a bundle of chemicals and viral attack when its body is incapable of throwing off such attacks.

The problems do not stop there. Many of these vaccines are targeted at very specific sites within the body where elements of the immune system will be present when the child's immune system develops. These kinds of vaccine can enter into these bodily sites and stay there whilst the immune system tissue grows around it. As the tissue grows, it has to incorporate the chemical residue from the vaccine and abnormalities can occur.

Two such sites are subject to attack by the diphtheria vaccine. The spinal column carries all of the information from the body to the brain via the central nervous system. At each vertebrae of the spine, nerves leave or enter the spinal cord, each nerve connecting to a specific region of the body. The nerves connecting to the lungs are located in the first five vertebrae of the neck counted from the junction with the spine (C7-C3). The nerves connecting with the ribs are located in most of the vertebrae of the upper back (T2-T11).

When the diphtheria vaccine is injected, it has nowhere to go as the infant does not have an immune system, so it finds its way into the spinal cord. The vaccine's make up is such that it is attracted to nerves which relate to the lungs and settles in the vertebrae of the two sites noted above. Once in place, it can begin to stimulate or even break down the nerves connected to the lungs and constant irritation results giving the child breathing difficulties. The vaccine can also make its way to the nerves connecting with the ribs, again causing irritation or damage.

One sixteen year old boy we treated for asthma began having attacks within days of being given the diphtheria vaccine as a child. His school had a policy of insisting that all children had their booster vaccinations and so several weeks before coming to see us he had his booster shot. Within a few days of the booster he had an asthma attack so severe that he had to be hospitalised for a week.

In all of the research we have done in recent years, we have found no hard evidence for health benefits from vaccination but we have found plenty of evidence of harm.

Another source of asthma type problems, in adults as well as children, which has a growing volume of evidence, is the dye used in margarines. When margarine has passed through its many production processes involving a large number of chemicals, it comes out as a grey mass which does not look very appetising. In order to market it, the grey gloop is coloured to look like a more natural product, butter. Different companies use different types of dye but most have been linked to asthma symptoms. The chemicals in the dye act in much the same way as the vaccine described above and migrate to the nerves controlling the function of the lungs with pretty much the same consequences.

Aspartame
Following on from our comments about the drug aspartame in Everything...etc., there has, at long last, been an interest shown by some newspapers. Here's one recent entry from our local paper, The Express and Echo, written by Alex Hendry under the headline "Diet drink sweetener in cancer probe".
"Scientists are to study possible links between an artificial sweetener used in many diet drinks and brain cancer, it was announced yesterday.

The three year study by researchers from King's College, London, will investigate whether the sweetener aspartame, marketed under the name of NutraAsweet, could be linked to an increased risk of primary brain tumours. NutraSweet, which is jointly owned by US giant Monsanto and Japanese company Ajinomoto, last night dismissed the proposed research as "scare mongering".

Company vice-president Hans Heezen said that they would be glad to have more evidence that the product was safe, but he added: "It seems that the money which has been allocated could be more usefully directed to other research projects."

The new research will be carried out by Dr Peter Nunn, a neurochemist, and Dr Geoff Pilkington. They will be trying to discover if one of the components of aspartame can attack DNA.

Dr Nunn said: "we are not suggesting that an entire population is at risk but it may be that certain groups with different genes are more susceptible to these compounds than others."

Aspartame breaks down into methanol, aspartic acid and phenylalaline. The last two are normal in people's daily diet. It is the effect of methanol that concerns some scientists."

Our research has shown that aspartame came to be used as an artificial sweetener about ten years ago when saccharine was linked to some forms of cancer and an alternative sweetener needed to be found as saccharine could no longer be marketed. Aspartame is a drug used in the treatment of stomach ulcers and is banned, as a sweetener, in ninety countries because of its adverse side effects. Ten years ago it was known that this drug had harmful side effects, this is why so many countries banned its use, yet we still have to wait a further three years before any British study is published. Although passed by the American FDA, the stories of its testing and passing we have heard could indicate that this organisation is not as infallible as most would like to think.

Many studies have been carried out into the safety of aspartame for sweetener use world wide and there are known to be a considerable number of very serious side effects, one of which is death, and yet it is still not banned world wide.

For our own curiosity we carried out our own poll into the contents of the soft drinks for sale on our local supermarket shelves. Over ninety percent of the drinks contained aspartame and about sixty percent contained aspartame and saccharine and most of these drinks were targeted directly at children.

New independent research reported on by Dr Russell Blaylock and published in Nexus Magazine in August/September 2000 goes into considerable medical detail of the effects of these kinds of substances on the brain, the central nervous system and the blood brain barrier. The report's conclusions are these:
"....Of particular concern are the toxic effects of these excitotoxic compounds on the developing brain. It is well recognised that the immature brain is four times more sensitive to the toxic effects of the excitatory amino acids as is the mature brain.

This means that excitotoxic injury is of special concern from the foetal stage to adolescence. There is evidence that the placenta concentrates several of these toxic amino acids on the foetal side of the placenta. Consumption of aspartame and MSG (monosodium glutamate) containing products by pregnant women during this critical period of brain formation is of special concern and should be discouraged.

Many of the effects, such as endocrine dysfunction and complex learning difficulties, are subtle and might not appear until the child is older. Other hypothalmic syndromes associated with excitotoxic lesions include immune alterations and violence dyscontrol.....There is sufficient medical literature documenting serious injury by these additives in the concentrations presently in our food supply to justify warning the public of these dangers. The case against aspartame is especially strong."

Need we say more?

Scientific Predictions
Well, we are into a new century and a new millennium and with the change of date came the usual crop of predictions about how science and technology is going to make our futures better.

For the past sixty years we have been inundated with these kinds of predictions. In years gone by, scientists have made promises like "by 1960 we will have eradicated cancer", "by 1970 we will be able to control weather", etc. One study carried out into all of these predictions for the last fifty years found that only about 1% of these predictions came about (source What Doctors Don't Tell You) and we still fall for them.

Have you noticed the most recent ones though? Virtually all of them contain the expression: "in ten years (or variable amount of years) it may be possible for scientists (or doctors) to........". What this expression actually means is that current scientific thinking leads them to believe that they have found a new area of research which they think might be profitable and they are looking for extra research funding to try out their pet theories. The statement are press releases attempting to maintain a high profile to attract funding, no more than that, other than maintaining a high publicity profile for scientific research and trying to continue the myth that the scientific community has the answer for all of humanity's ills.

Scientists are very good at describing what is happening in their experiments but not very good at understanding what is happening in their experiments and this is why only about 1% of their predictions actually come true. We support scientific research, we just wish that scientists would learn to see properly and not bend the truth to suit whoever happens to be paying their wages.

Scientific research and conclusions really do seem to be out of control, the thought processes behind many scientific statements are baffling.

On the 11th February 2000 (it was not April 1st), the BBC international television news carried an item which stated that scientists now believe that many childhood illnesses and adult health problems stem from the fact that we keep our children in a world which is far too sanitised. Traditionally, children have played out of doors and in mud etc. where they have slowly been exposed to a huge variety of bacteria. When these bacteria invade the body, the immune system learns to fight and become very strong, building up resources to fight any future health problem. Most children are now kept indoors where they are not exposed to these bacteria and their immune systems do not build up sufficient experience and strength in fighting infection and disease. An extremely common sense piece of scientific research, and a position which we have stated on many occasions in the past few years.

The scientific answer to this problem? They are developing a vaccination which contains most of the common bacteria to be injected into children at a very early age. Instead of normal, healthy childhood development they are proposing yet another bundle of chemicals to inject, but this time, they are specifically designed to attack a child's immune system. This proposal would have doctors inject all of the bacteria into the child in one go at a time when the child does not have an immune system to fight off such attacks. This can only cause more damage (see the item on asthma above).

In a world which is increasingly sanitised there are a large variety of products coming onto the market which are described as being "antibacterial". The purpose of these products is to try to eliminate bacteria from just about any surface within the home.

There is only one way for a product to be described in this way and that is because it contains one or more chemical pesticides. Every time you spray something with an antibacterial spray, wipe a surface with an antibacterial wipe, wash dishes in an antibacterial washing up liquid, you are adding pesticides to the surface. One very commonly used pesticide is organo-phosphate.

Our views on this substance, and its link with BSE and CJD, were discussed in *Everything......etc.* but new research shows other problems. As we write, the Ministry of Agriculture is holding inquiries into evidence of the link between BSE in cattle and organo-phosphates. As part of these meetings the following report was handed to the ministry and broadcast on BBC news on the 29th March 2000 under the headline of: "Pesticides Linked To Baby Heart Defects".

"New research has linked a chemical found in pesticides to heart defects and learning difficulties in babies.
Scientists have revealed that health problems were found in babies born to twelve mothers exposed to organo-phosphates during the early stages of pregnancy.

The chemical is found in products including sheep dip and fly spray. The study was revealed at a Ministry of Agriculture meeting according to the BBC's Farming Today programme".

Where is the advertising campaign for antibacterial (pesticide containing) products aimed? That's right, pregnant women and young families!

Whilst on the subject of strange substances being medically introduced into the body, here's a report that appeared on the 16th February 2000 on BBC Ceefax.
"HRT HIGH BREAST CANCER RISK - NEW STUDY"

"Combined Hormone Replacement Therapy (HRT) increases the risk of breast cancer by 24% for every five years taken, new research suggests.

Oestrogen only HRT increases the risk by 6% for every year taken says University of Southern California experts in their "definitive" study.

A total of 3500 US women were interviewed during the research.

The study is published in the National Cancer Institutes Journal".

One thing about scientific reports is that if it shows up a treatment or a drug in a bad light, the research will have been checked to an infinite degree to ensure that they cannot be sued by the drug companies.

Women
In putting this book together, we read through a number of year's worth of client notes and two things stood out as being the greatest causes of health problems in women.
The first is giving birth.

So many women we see have back, pelvis and hip problems. To accommodate a growing fetus, a woman's pelvis hinges on the sacro/illiac joint at the base of the spine. After giving

190

birth, the joint should return to its normal position. However, if the mother is feeling a little insecure after the birth (which the vast majority of women will be) the joint does not return properly and if there are any insecurities within her relationship with the father, the problem can become much worse. The situation leads to the base of the spine becoming a little unstable and the spine itself put into an unnatural curve leading to many years of back pain.

A second effect is that with a weakness within this joint, the pelvis is no longer a level, stable platform to take the weight of the upper body and distribute it evenly into the legs. With a tilt on the pelvis, a larger proportion of the weight is placed onto one or other hip joint and, over the years, the hip joint wears away leading to a hip replacement operation and all of the problems associated with those kinds of operations.

If, after giving birth, a woman consults a sacro/cranial practitioner or an osteopath, these bones can be gently placed back into their correct position preventing many years of back pain and potential surgery (hip replacement) 40 years in the future.

The second biggest cause of problems with women is blocked lymphatic tissue.

The lymphatic system is almost as extensive as the blood circulation system. It is part of the body's immune system and drains any unwanted substances out of the body keeping the body as smoothly functioning and disease free as possible. If this system becomes blocked, toxins, viruses, bacteria, etc. become held within the body and a variety of health problems can result. The body's lymphatic system is controlled by two separate chakras and two separate organs.

The lower body's lymph tissue is controlled by the spleen. This is an organ about the size of a clenched fist, tucked away behind the stomach and up against the diaphragm. It has several functions within the body but the one most usually affected with women is its lymph drainage function.

The spleen relates to the third chakra (personal power and emotions) with the specific role of dealing with the frustrations of life, especially frustrations linked with suppressed anger.

Most women's lives are mapped out by society into various stages; they are someone's daughter, someone's girlfriend, someone's mother, they are very rarely allowed to be themselves. This builds up a great deal of frustration with most women. Add to this situation the everyday frustrations with partners, children, schools, doctors, hospitals, supermarket queues, etc. etc. and you end up with a lower body lymphatic system which begins to block as all of the accumulated frustration prevents the proper functioning of the spleen. All of this leads to the formation of cellulite; weight around the abdomen and thighs which does not respond to any diet; psoriasis (especially to the legs) and, ultimately, conditions such as diverticulitis, Crohn's disease and even bowel cancer.

The only effective way of dealing with these kinds of problems is to remove the frustrations out of the system. This is not usually that easy in day to day life and so the best way is through the "giveaway". This involves writing down all of your frustrations, angers, emotions onto paper on a regular basis and, when you have finished writing a section, tear it up and either throw it in the bin or, best still, burn it. Do not read back what you have written before ripping it up as that can put all of the emotions back into your system. Just write it, tear it up and dispose of it. The process sounds very simplistic, but it can be extremely effective. Give it a go, you have nothing to lose except a lifetimes worth of emotional baggage.

The other chakra and organ which controls the lymph system is the fourth, heart chakra and the thymus gland.

The thymus gland controls the function of the upper body lymphatic system. The fourth chakra is all about how we express our feelings of love, either towards others or towards ourselves. By expressions of love towards ourselves we mean our sense of self worth, how we see ourselves as a person.

For the social reasons given above, women are not allowed to have an opinion of themselves. They must always put themselves back by seeing to everyone else's needs first. If a woman begins to look after herself and her needs, she is considered selfish. These actions and attitudes lead to the upper body lymphatic system becoming blocked as the thymus gland becomes blocked with all of the woman's unexpressed self. Problems that can arise from the thymus blocking are situations such as a tendency to hold infections in place; fungal infections; headaches; earache; tinnitus; breast lumps; tender lumps under the armpits and, ultimately, breast cancer.

The best way of dealing with this kind of situation is to begin to look at your life and all of your successes. Just surviving your life can be a cause for celebration. If you have children, look at how they have grown up, you were mainly responsible for their coming safely through their early years. Look around at where you live, you were probable responsible for making it a home. Look at where you work, the work that you have done has helped the company to survive. These are all ways of honouring yourself.

Think of how you felt when you did something creative, when your child achieved something, when you wrote your first professional letter, when you passed an exam, when you got the job you wanted - all achievements that you achieved. Recognise the role that you have played in achieving the things you have achieved in your life - they are your successes and you should honour yourself for them. This is what clears the thymus. It does not make you egotistical or selfish, it just brings some balance back into your life and to your heart - reread case forty four at the start of the last chapter.

There is nothing wrong in helping other people, just remember that you are worth something too.

You can also try having a lymph drainage massage. These can be quite painful if the lymphs are badly blocked, but it is one of the best ways of cleansing the lymphatic system, both upper and lower halves, and bringing some life back to your body. It can also help reduce weight, infections, headaches and cellulite and, by giving yourself the treat of a massage as a gift to yourself, it helps to clear the thymus gland and energise the heart chakra. There are also a number of herbs which are very good at clearing out the lymph system - go and see a herbalist.

Oh, and don't forget to give yourself as many treats as possible - you are worth it!

Chocolate
You all think that chocolate is unhealthy, causes fat and causes spots. Wrong.

Chocolate is made from the cocoa bean and has been used over many thousands of years as the drink of the gods. It has been claimed that chocolate can raise the psyche to transcend the physical or stimulate the brain into mimicking an orgasm. Its all true. As healers, we always recommend to our healing pupils that they carry a bar of chocolate with them to help revive their energies after giving a healing session - it always works.

Chocolate is a primary antioxidant. It has more antioxidant ingredients per unit weight than virtually any other substance known to man (this is solid organic bar chocolate made in the traditional way and not the vegetable based form the EU is currently considering).

Chocolate acts within the body's lymphatic system as a major cleanser. The lymph system removes unwanted substances such as toxins and bacteria from the body's tissues. The lymphs then drain into the blood for removal from the body. The lymphs in the upper body drain into the thymus gland and the lower body lymphs into the spleen. If the function of these organs is impaired in any way, the lymphs can block causing a back up within the system. Chocolate acts as a cleanser for the lymphs by breaking down the lymph contents into something more easily cleared.

If the lower lymphs are blocked by the spleen not functioning fully (too much frustration in your life), the active ingredient in chocolate makes the lymph tissue swell giving the appearance of weight gain. If the upper body lymph tissue is blocked by the thymus not functioning fully (not enough self honouring), the lymphs can drain in the opposite direction and give you spots.

So, it isn't the chocolate that's the problem, its the life you live that stops the chocolate doing its job.

Eat organic chocolate, it's good for you.

Even the doctors are coming out on our side!
Here's a report from 19th February 2000 on BBC Ceefax.
"Chocolate Good For The Heart: New Study"

"Chocolate could be good for the heart, a preliminary study has suggested.

Moderate chocolate consumption can improve blood and platelet function, said Carl Keen, professor of nutrition at the University of California, Davis.

"He said chocolate is thought to contain a high level of flavanoids, naturally occurring plant compounds that boost blood flow.

The study of forty people showed that chocolate boosted the heart like aspirin."

We know which we would prefer to take if it came to a straight choice between aspirin or chocolate and it wouldn't be aspirin!

Having said all of that about chocolate, if you want to be scared silly, read up on the evidence of damage caused to the body (especially children) by refined white sugars! If you must use sugar, use unrefined raw cane sugar, especially an organic brand (the kind used to make organic chocolate - another good reason to only eat organic chocolate!).

*****

After all of the evidence we have presented in this book, it should be clear by now that good health is not an accident but in the control of everyone to achieve. Regardless of the state of your health or the symptoms of illness you are experiencing, by taking responsibility for the root causes of YOUR illness, YOU can undo all of the problems and bring your body back to a state of balance. No illness is beyond the point of no return.

Be yourself and drop all of the masks that you have built up over the years but, most importantly of all

HAVE FUN!

196

Other healing books from Capall Bann Publishing

The Healing Book   Chris Thomas & Diane Baker

"The exercises are well described and arranged in a good order of development, clearly relevant case examples..a good basic book written in plain English by two clearly competent healers keen on sharing their knowledge" Touchstone

This book is for those who wish to heal, starting at the beginning of the healing process with simple, easily followed exercises which can begin to unlock the healing potential which is inherent in all of us. Nobody needs to feel left out of these abilities. We are all healers, all that we need to do is to stop telling ourselves that we are not. Whatever level of experience you have of healing, this book explains in simple uncomplicated language that does not use mysticism or any form of ritual, how to understand the "Chakras" and the way in which our daily lives influence them, to relate medical conditions to the chakras and to learn methods which will bring the chakras back into balance, both for yourself and for others. These methods apply equally to humans and to animals. If you do not have any experience of giving healing, but would like to learn, this book can set you on that path. If you already work as a healer, in whatever capacity, and would like to explore your greater potential, this book is also for you. The authors have a combined experience of over twenty five years of providing healing and have taught very many people to unlock their own healing potential. This book is not only about learning to heal from the beginning, but also explores some of the energy manipulation techniques used by the authors in their daily practise as "Psychic Surgeons". An accompanying tape is available from the authors.
ISBN 186163 053 0   £8.95

Everything You Always Wanted To Know About Your Body, But, So Far, Nobody's Been Able To Tell You   Chris Thomas & Diane Baker

"...easy to understand...insight into how you can heal yourself...comprehensive guide" Here's Health

Have you ever wondered why some people become ill and others do not? Why some people recover from illness and others do not? Do you know how your body really works? Why do diets rarely work? Is there an alternative approach to treating symptoms of illness instead of using prescriptive drugs? Well here is a book which leads you through the body, organ by organ, system by system, and explains in clear language how illness arises and what to do about it. The first half of the book fully explains the workings of the human body in simple language and clear illustrations. It explains which elements are connected together and why they can influence each other. It also relates each region and organ to its associated chakra and how our day-to-day lives have an influence on our health and well-being. Every part of the body is dealt with in these ways and the major underlying causes for most of our illnesses explained. It also provides details and suggestions on how to heal yourself by working on the root cause issues. This book also takes a look at how some illnesses are brought about by past life traumas. The second half of the book looks at ways of healing the symptoms of illness without the need for prescriptive drugs. Several forms of healing practices are used to achieve this: Bach Flower Remedies, Reflexology, Herbalism, Biochemic Tissue Salts and Homeopathy are the main approaches used, with a further twenty seven therapies fully described. This is an extensive, comprehensive look at the body and illness. It is also one of the most comprehensive guides to alternative treatments currently available.
ISBN 186163 098 0   £17.95

The Journey Home   Chris Thomas

Who are we? Why are we here? Are we alone? What relationship does Earth and its multitude of lifeforms have to themselves and to the universe? The answers to many of these questions have long been available, but over the centuries they have become hidden by personal interests and clouded by repetition and dogma. As we undergo a vast shift in consciousness, the underlying reasons for our existence have to be rediscovered and put into their proper perspective. This book brings these issues into a sharper focus and sheds light into some of the darker corners. Gone are the dark days of Karmic re-cycling and suffering; we have reached the time of the birth of a new human existence so far removed from human experience that most have not yet recognised its coming. ISBN 186163 041 7   £7.95

The Fool's First Steps   Chris Thomas

"much that makes sense...on a deeper level" Prediction

Are you asking Questions? Transforming? Wanting to know the purpose of it all? Do the old answers no longer work?   The true purposes of Avebury and Stonehenge and the knowledge contained there, stellar gateways, the origins of crop circles, changing Earth energies, the true nature of angels... Personal transformations happening now on a grand scale, mental, emotional and physical. Realising the spiritual origins of the human race... If this book were a novel it would make fascinating reading, but as the explanations again and again strike a true chord, it makes compulsive and unforgettable reading which will help you change how you view life. ISBN 186163 072 7   £9.95

Planet Earth - The Universe's Experiment

Chris Thomas

Who are we? Where do we come from? What is our purpose and why did we go wrong? Humans are not of the Earth but have arrived on this planet to explore. On our joyous arrival we encountered the spirits of the land, the Sidhe and the faerie. As we became more human we began to lose our memories of our origins and the knowledge of our true purpose andf potential. As we approach the completion of our climb back to reality, we are awakening the ghosts of this knowledge. Lemuria, Atlantis, the thirteen races have all played their part in "The Human Plan", all are now working to assist us to our chosen goal - full consciousness. But, time is short and unless we complete our journey soon, the Earth will be lost to us. Virtually all our experience and history is at odds with the archaeological and scientific versions of our past, only the Akashic tells the real history. What is told here is the Akashic's story.

ISBN 186163 224X   £11.95

Healing Journeys   Paul Williamson

Paul Williamson is a Past Life Therapist, Hypnotherapist and Healer. Here, he tells about his own unfolding spiritual path and what he has discovered about past lives, healing the inner child, channelling, spiritual healing and earth healing. Using numerous case studies, Paul shares his approaches to therapy and methods of healing that have helped people from their inner experiences to find peace and well-being. Within these stories, Paul charts some fascinating possibilities about the nature of our inner reality. From this, Paul affirms the relevance and importance of honouring the inner spiritual dimension of our being, so that if we can find peace within, then this could help us find greater meaning in our external lives, and help us to create a happier, healthier society too. Told simply and from the heart, this book shares many touching human and spiritual experiences that will interest seekers everywhere. These experiences can be truly called "Healing Journeys". ISBN 186163 100 6   £11.95

FREE DETAILED CATALOGUE

Capall Bann is owned and run by people actively involved in many of the areas in which we publish. A detailed illustrated catalogue is available on request, SAE or International Postal Coupon appreciated. **Titles can be ordered direct from Capall Bann, post free in the UK** (cheque or PO with order) or from good bookshops and specialist outlets.

Do contact us for details on the latest releases at: **Capall Bann Publishing, Auton Farm, Milverton, Somerset, TA4 1NE.** Titles include:

A Breath Behind Time, Terri Hector
Angels and Goddesses - Celtic Christianity & Paganism, M. Howard
Arthur - The Legend Unveiled, C Johnson & E Lung
Astrology The Inner Eye - A Guide in Everyday Language, E Smith
Auguries and Omens - The Magical Lore of Birds, Yvonne Aburrow
Asyniur - Womens Mysteries in the Northern Tradition, S McGrath
Beginnings - Geomancy, Builder's Rites & Electional Astrology in the
    European Tradition, Nigel Pennick
Between Earth and Sky, Julia Day
Book of the Veil , Peter Paddon
Caer Sidhe - Celtic Astrology and Astronomy, Vol 1, Michael Bayley
Caer Sidhe - Celtic Astrology and Astronomy, Vol 2 M Bayley
Call of the Horned Piper, Nigel Jackson
Cat's Company, Ann Walker
Celtic Faery Shamanism, Catrin James
Celtic Faery Shamanism - The Wisdom of the Otherworld, Catrin James
Celtic Lore & Druidic Ritual, Rhiannon Ryall
Celtic Sacrifice - Pre Christian Ritual & Religion, Marion Pearce
Celtic Saints and the Glastonbury Zodiac, Mary Caine
Circle and the Square, Jack Gale
Compleat Vampyre - The Vampyre Shaman, Nigel Jackson
Creating Form From the Mist - The Wisdom of Women in Celtic Myth and
    Culture, Lynne Sinclair-Wood
Crystal Clear - A Guide to Quartz Crystal, Jennifer Dent
Crystal Doorways, Simon & Sue Lilly
Crossing the Borderlines - Guising, Masking & Ritual Animal Disguise in the
    European Tradition, Nigel Pennick
Dragons of the West, Nigel Pennick
Earth Dance - A Year of Pagan Rituals, Jan Brodie
Earth Harmony - Places of Power, Holiness & Healing, Nigel Pennick
Earth Magic, Margaret McArthur

Eildon Tree (The) Romany Language & Lore, Michael Hoadley
Enchanted Forest - The Magical Lore of Trees, Yvonne Aburrow
Eternal Priestess, Sage Weston
Eternally Yours Faithfully, Roy Radford & Evelyn Gregory
Everything You Always Wanted To Know About Your Body, But So Far
	Nobody's Been Able To Tell You, Chris Thomas & D Baker
Face of the Deep - Healing Body & Soul, Penny Allen
Fairies in the Irish Tradition, Molly Gowen
Familiars - Animal Powers of Britain, Anna Franklin
Fool's First Steps, (The) Chris Thomas
Forest Paths - Tree Divination, Brian Harrison, Ill. S. Rouse
From Past to Future Life, Dr Roger Webber
Gardening For Wildlife Ron Wilson
God Year, The, Nigel Pennick & Helen Field
Goddess on the Cross, Dr George Young
Goddess Year, The, Nigel Pennick & Helen Field
Goddesses, Guardians & Groves, Jack Gale
Handbook For Pagan Healers, Liz Joan
Handbook of Fairies, Ronan Coghlan
Healing Book, The, Chris Thomas and Diane Baker
Healing Homes, Jennifer Dent
Healing Journeys, Paul Williamson
Healing Stones, Sue Philips
Herb Craft - Shamanic & Ritual Use of Herbs, Lavender & Franklin
Hidden Heritage - Exploring Ancient Essex, Terry Johnson
Hub of the Wheel, Skytoucher
In Search of Herne the Hunter, Eric Fitch
Inner Celtia, Alan Richardson & David Annwn
Inner Mysteries of the Goths, Nigel Pennick
Inner Space Workbook - Develop Thru Tarot, C Summers & J Vayne
Intuitive Journey, Ann Walker Isis - African Queen, Akkadia Ford
Journey Home, The, Chris Thomas
Kecks, Keddles & Kesh - Celtic Lang & The Cog Almanac, Bayley
Language of the Psycards, Berenice
Legend of Robin Hood, The, Richard Rutherford-Moore
Lid Off the Cauldron, Patricia Crowther
Light From the Shadows - Modern Traditional Witchcraft, Gwyn
Living Tarot, Ann Walker
Lore of the Sacred Horse, Marion Davies
Lost Lands & Sunken Cities (2nd ed.), Nigel Pennick
Magic of Herbs - A Complete Home Herbal, Rhiannon Ryall
Magical Guardians - Exploring the Spirit and Nature of Trees, Philip Heselton
Magical History of the Horse, Janet Farrar & Virginia Russell
Magical Lore of Animals, Yvonne Aburrow
Magical Lore of Cats, Marion Davies
Magical Lore of Herbs, Marion Davies

Magick Without Peers, Ariadne Rainbird & David Rankine
Masks of Misrule - Horned God & His Cult in Europe, Nigel Jackson
Medicine For The Coming Age, Lisa Sand MD
Medium Rare - Reminiscences of a Clairvoyant, Muriel Renard
Menopausal Woman on the Run, Jaki da Costa
Mind Massage - 60 Creative Visualisations, Marlene Maundrill
Mirrors of Magic - Evoking the Spirit of the Dewponds, P Heselton
Moon Mysteries, Jan Brodie
Mysteries of the Runes, Michael Howard
Mystic Life of Animals, Ann Walker
New Celtic Oracle The, Nigel Pennick & Nigel Jackson
Oracle of Geomancy, Nigel Pennick
Pagan Feasts - Seasonal Food for the 8 Festivals, Franklin & Phillips
Patchwork of Magic - Living in a Pagan World, Julia Day
Pathworking - A Practical Book of Guided Meditations, Pete Jennings
Personal Power, Anna Franklin
Pickingill Papers - The Origins of Gardnerian Wicca, Bill Liddell
Pillars of Tubal Cain, Nigel Jackson
Places of Pilgrimage and Healing, Adrian Cooper
Practical Divining, Richard Foord
Practical Meditation, Steve Hounsome
Practical Spirituality, Steve Hounsome
Psychic Self Defence - Real Solutions, Jan Brodie
Real Fairies, David Tame
Reality - How It Works & Why It Mostly Doesn't, Rik Dent
Romany Tapestry, Michael Houghton
Runic Astrology, Nigel Pennick
Sacred Animals, Gordon MacLellan
Sacred Celtic Animals, Marion Davies, Ill. Simon Rouse
Sacred Dorset - On the Path of the Dragon, Peter Knight
Sacred Grove - The Mysteries of the Forest, Yvonne Aburrow
Sacred Geometry, Nigel Pennick
Sacred Nature, Ancient Wisdom & Modern Meanings, A Cooper
Sacred Ring - Pagan Origins of British Folk Festivals, M. Howard
Season of Sorcery - On Becoming a Wisewoman, Poppy Palin
Seasonal Magic - Diary of a Village Witch, Paddy Slade
Secret Places of the Goddess, Philip Heselton
Secret Signs & Sigils, Nigel Pennick
Self Enlightenment, Mayan O'Brien
Spirits of the Air, Jaq D Hawkins
Spirits of the Earth, Jaq D Hawkins
Spirits of the Earth, Jaq D Hawkins
Stony Gaze, Investigating Celtic Heads John Billingsley
Stumbling Through the Undergrowth , Mark Kirwan-Heyhoe
Subterranean Kingdom, The, revised 2nd ed, Nigel Pennick
Symbols of Ancient Gods, Rhiannon Ryall

Talking to the Earth, Gordon MacLellan
Taming the Wolf - Full Moon Meditations, Steve Hounsome
Teachings of the Wisewomen, Rhiannon Ryall
The Other Kingdoms Speak, Helena Hawley
Tree: Essence of Healing, Simon & Sue Lilly
Tree: Essence, Spirit & Teacher, Simon & Sue Lilly
Through the Veil, Peter Paddon
Torch and the Spear, Patrick Regan
Understanding Chaos Magic, Jaq D Hawkins
Vortex - The End of History, Mary Russell
Warp and Weft - In Search of the I-Ching, William de Fancourt
Warriors at the Edge of Time, Jan Fry
Water Witches, Tony Steele
Way of the Magus, Michael Howard
Weaving a Web of Magic, Rhiannon Ryall
West Country Wicca, Rhiannon Ryall
Wildwitch - The Craft of the Natural Psychic, Poppy Palin
Wildwood King , Philip Kane
Witches of Oz, Matthew & Julia Philips
Wondrous Land - The Faery Faith of Ireland by Dr Kay Mullin
Working With the Merlin, Geoff Hughes
Your Talking Pet, Ann Walker

FREE detailed catalogue and FREE 'Inspiration' magazine

Contact: Capall Bann Publishing, Auton Farm, Milverton, Somerset, TA4 1NE